Transformation Magic Megabook

The Original One Page Series

Ken Martin

Copyright

Dedication

This book is dedicated to my amazing boys Jack and Jake.

Contents

Contents

Contents

Preface

I have always been interested in effective communications and the art of making the complex simple. This approach is a primary goal of 3 Magic Publications, which I have founded to facilitate successful business change and transformation by using innovative and creative documentation to communicate key messages and best practices.

During my career, I wanted a reference method of best practices at my fingertips, where, instead of reading numerous self-development, management and technical books, I could have a handy one-page cheat sheet. So, I developed the "One Page Magic" – the idea of having one book on a page. This print edition is a new format to facilitate the print edition, I hope you find this new format useful as the classic one-page grid format.

Ken Martin

Introduction

How to read

This book comprises experience and best practices that cover all aspects of being successful in planning and implementing Business Transformations for an enhanced Customer Experience.

Why use best practices

There is a well-known phrase - "Keep doing the same things and expecting different results is a sign of insanity". Yet this is what many people and companies continue to do by doing the same things, making the same mistakes and expecting different results. But how many project managers have recorded lessons learned and even more rare how many project managers have read lessons learned from other's experiences of previous projects.

Best practices often derived from lessons learned and hard-earned experience can save you a lot of wasted effort, time and often failure. They can contribute to your success in all aspects of initiatives, projects and life. Learn from other's best practices of experiences and avoid common mistakes & succeed the first time.

THE CREATION OF A THOUSAND

FORESTS IS ONE ACORN.

Ralph Waldo Emerson

01 Leading a digital transformation

Technology, data, process, and organizational change all play a role in business transformation. Increased adaptability and agility are required in the contemporary workplace. Companies must move quickly to deal with immediate disruptions while also laying the groundwork for long-term success.

Leaders are reconsidering their operational procedures, including how to accomplish global business and digital transformation, to have the most impact possible on their top and bottom lines, to adopt a global business to the remote and virtual workforce. Before a leader can alter an organization, they must first define the existing situation and then make plans for the future. It enables them to analyse what is now doable as well as see the gaps that will require investment and change to close.

Companies must combine a clear view and understanding of external disruptors such as market trends, technology, government regulations, talent availability, and generational differences with a focus on culture, leadership, technology adoption, and organisational design to achieve transformational fitness. Cloud and mobile technologies, for example, have blurred the borders between business and personal life by allowing people to work whenever and from wherever they wish.

If the organization is open to remote working, employees can communicate with anyone in any time zone. As a result, company data and applications are now expected to be accessible 24 hours a day, seven days a week. Driving objectives are just as important as establishing and accomplishing them when it comes to strategic change and it needs an assigned senior leader authorized and accountable for its success.

THE CREATION OF A THE LESS

ONE HAS TO DO, THE LESS

TIME ONE FINDS TO DO IT IN.

Lord Chesterfield

Key questions for a transformation (1)

Problems to solve
Why do we exist, what problems do we solve & what do we do best?

Alignment with strategy
How does the transformation program align with strategy?

Key players in strategy
Who should be involved in developing the strategy?

Guiding principles
What is the strategy guiding principles?

Business goals
What are the transformation business goals and solution vision?

Priorities & outcomes
What are the important priorities & what are the desired outcomes?

Customer experience
How will the transformation enhance the customer experience?

Revenue drivers
What parts of the business are our biggest revenue drivers?

Transformation risks
What are the risks of transforming the business?

Business agility
Is the organisation agile enough for a successful transformation?

Key questions for a transformation (2)

Biggest impact

Which business areas would have the biggest impact?

Roles & responsibilities

What are the roles and responsibilities for the transformation?

Transformation budgets

Are budgets aligned with transformation initiatives?

Employees' productivity

How will the vision's goal increase employees' productivity?

Business processes

What changes are required to internal business processes?

Creativity & collaboration

How to create an environment for greater creativity & collaboration?

Platforms & tools

What are the platforms and tools required for the transformation?

Success metrics

How will success be measured and what could be the metrics?

Training & new skills

What training and new skills will be required?

The success factors for a transformation

Communication of change

Leadership who can communicate the transformation change journey and its benefits to the company and its staff and gain alignment on a common purpose going forward.

An integrated, agile approach

Taking an integrated and iterative agile approach that brings transformational change to people, processes and systems is a path towards successful business transformation.

Transformation PMO

Having a transformation PMO responsible for driving complex initiatives of the strategy of the organisation. It is a critical link between the executive vision and the work of the enterprise. Effective Project Management and Risk Management is required to deliver transformation initiatives to achieve the desired outcomes

Customer centric vision

The Business Transformation needs to be a customer-centric vision.

Value add service

Managing change cannot be underestimated with transformation initiatives. There needs to be an effective change communications plan about the coming changes.

Quick wins

Leadership needs to build a culture of agility and adaptability that facilitates innovation and collaboration, the acceptance of change and new and different ways of working.

Continuous improvement

A key to successful transformation is having the the right talents and skills.

Not technology focused

Technology choices should be based on the potential value add enhancements to customer experience, operations, products and services.

The desired state for a transformation

A clear purpose

Leaders have a clear purpose for transformation. They have an attitude of asking: "why?"

Best practices adopted

Best practices are implemented for global remote and virtual teams, allowing anyone to work anywhere and anytime with increased collaboration.

Processes transformed

A big focus on reinventing business processes to lower costs, reduce cycle times, and increase quality using new technology.

An agile organization

The organization is agile by understanding that true transformation (learning, flexibility, autonomy) is required for sustainable transformation.

Customer experience focus

The external focus is on the customer experience.

A holistic framework

A holistic set of platforms, tools and environments for work delivered in a usable and coherent way.

Technology use to transform

Using digital technologies to transform existing processes to become more efficient and to transform that service into something significantly better.

Access data anywhere, anytime

Allowing employees to access data in real-time and from any location.

Increased efficiency

Streamlined operations with digital workplaces operating at peak capacity; saving money & time and making staff training more efficient..

GIVE ME 6 HOURS TO CHOP DOWN
A TREE AND I WILL SPEND THE
FIRST 4 SHARPENING THE AXE.

Abraham Lincoln

Leading a digital transformation

Why is transformation difficult?

Too much focus on technology
Too often the focus is on technology, with little to no thought about the process itself

A lack of effectiveness leveraging data
DT is hard as it is about how effective the organization is at leveraging data to digitalize their business model & its value

Not really a transformation
After the DT project, the character of the business does not change, it still does business as usual

A lack of knowing what transformation is...
There is a lack of knowing what DT means to an Organization's customers, partners, channels and employees

Insufficient CEO leadership
An issue often highlighted by staff of digital transformation is insufficient CEO leadership

Too much focus on 'ASIS" processes
Too much focus on optimising ASIS processes & not enough focus on mapping business model to customer's value creation

What is digital transformation?

Process transformation
A big focus to reinvent processes with the goal of lowering costs, reducing cycle times, or using new technology

Business model transformation
Business's are looking to see how to transform the basic building blocks their business model and how value is delivered in their sector

Domain transformation
Business's are recognising that industry limits are becoming blurred with new tech that are creating new types of competitors

Organization transformation
Agile Organizations understand that true transformation (learning, flexibility, autonomy) is required for sustainable transformation

Reasons for failure

- No business case for transformation
- no capabilities to drive innovation
- no sense of urgency to make investments
- A lack of CEO/ board sponsorship
- No focus on projects that impact business
- Existing IT systems can't support transformation

Qualities needed to lead a digital transformation

Have a clear purpose going forward
They have an attitude of asking why? Are we adding technology to remain competitive, create a more productive workforce

Always looking for the next opportunity
Successful digital leaders think ahead, always searching for the next opportunity today, tomorrow and in the future

Fixing things that are broken and not right
Digital leaders fix what's broken and for what is not right. & will drive team problem solving, decision making & collaboration

Digital leaders are risk takers and experimenters
Digital leaders are risk-takers & experimenters who foster a culture for experimentation & innovation, out of failure comes success

Digital leaders strive for collaborative partnerships
A digital leader knows collaborations across the enterprise is key to be successful & isn't afraid of embracing collaborative partnerships

What is business disruption?

Disruption = process
Disruption is a process, not a product or service, that occurs from the fringe to mainstream

Originates new markets
Originate in low-end (less demanding customers) or new market footholds

Quality standards
New firms don't catch on with primary customers until quality catches up with their standards

Some disrupters fail
Success is not a requirement for disruptors and some business can be disruptive but fail anyway

Different business model
New firm's business model differs significantly from incumbent business's business model

The challenges of digital transformation

Employee pushback
Changes makes staff alarmed but in the digital age not changing is riskier

A digital strategy
A firm must have a digital strategy with a vision, set goals & direction for it

Requires the right people
DT brings with it many technical challenges & a needs digital skilled people

Requires flexibility
DT needs a fluid company structure for new tech, data & customer focus

Manage budget
Have a plan over several phases. Don't risk firm over budgetary issues

Digital transformation elements

- Customer perception & touch points
- Sales proposition
- Performance management
- Automation
- Visualizing work
- Digitising the business
- New digital products
- Digital Globalization

02 Transformation to remote teams

Increased adaptability and agility are required in the contemporary workplace. Companies must move quickly to deal with immediate disruptions while also laying the groundwork for long-term success. A shift to a remote workforce necessitates a shift in thinking. Leadership must place a premium on putting their people's trust in them. Offering more autonomy, entrusting individual and team decisions, boosting transparency through stronger communication skills, and holding people accountable for their results are all examples of this.

Regardless of borders or time zones, global business and digital transformation enable everyone to operate anywhere, at any time, with enhanced productivity and adaptability. When working remotely, communication and collaboration are critical, but they can be easily disrupted when moving from an office to a remote location. Fortunately, there are a variety of platforms that may be swiftly implemented and provide significant assistance.

A key component of any high-functioning remote collaboration is consistent communication. Managers may establish a culture where employees feel heard, keep productive, and are accountable even when they are far away by asking questions frequently. Businesses are encouraging virtual teams to be more creative, innovative, and collaborative by educating team members on how to use relationship-building skills and trust even when they are not in the same room.

Employees who are separated from their office and team may feel disconnected from the organization's wider mission and goals. Regular meetings, which can be conducted over the phone or by video conference, can assist managers to understand what projects their staff are working on, where they are stuck, and what they have accomplished.

WELL DONE IS BETTER THAN WELL SAID.

Benjamin Franklin

Transformation to remote teams

Strategies to implement transformation to global remote teams

Remote implementation roadmap
- Establish planning cycle, phases, approach
- Define comms vehicles & channels, timings
- Determine feedback mechanism
- Educate guide leaders and teams

Deliver right message
- What's happening
- Why it's happening
- How change will affect all teams
- What is needed to make change

Collaboration platforms
- Establish interactive collaboration tools
- Foster transparent culture of CI
- Ensure work hours overlap
- Create meritocratic system for rewards

Create successful workgroups
- Establish work guidelines
- Define business processes & models
- Ensure Measurable deliverables
- Create open & transparent environs

Transition
- Assign virtual implementation teams
- Create detailed execution plans
- Train people in new environs
- Reconfigure systems

Implement
- Implement new governance
- Monitor progress, adoption, trends

Evaluate
- Assess results vs. scorecard
- Encourage continuous feedback

Process / governance frameworks

Adapt processes and governance models
- Design fluid and flexible processes aligned to a remote-based strategy & business goals

Communication and training
- Communicate the new processes & business rules and provide required one-on-one & self-paced training in skills to achieve business results

Introduce new business rules
- Determine remote work schedule, work roles, meetings and comms policies

Support
- Provide continuous support to ensure all remote teams understand & adapt to new remote-based work policies

Establish clear tracking measures
- Develop clear KPIs for productivity, transparency & accountable for tasks & projects

Review, evaluate and improve
- Assess remote teams' understanding of roles, responsibilities & expectations under new processes & rules, conduct frequent surveys

Risk management and change monitoring

Conduct change mgt. and risk assessment
- Establish the scope of risk assessment (change impact assessment)

Use different assessment methods
- Use different risk assessment techniques, inc. statistical probability assessments, benchmarking, interviews, focus groups, conceptualizations, impact matrix analysis

Analyse current business processes
- Identify gaps & causes for improving productivity, effectiveness & efficiency

Categorise potential risks
- Group potential risks into high, medium, low risk scenarios. Assess impacts to organization, stakeholder groups, products (if applicable), ASIS to TOBE scenarios

Identify business opportunities
- Identify & validate opportunities to act on analysis results to identify transformation opportunities

Leadership commitment and monitor progress
- Ensure leadership commitment to change
- Monitor progress, implementation, impact, required ongoing support, required training, potential resistance & potential employee disengagement

Virtual meetings, communications & collaboration

Use interactive forums and portals
- Use interactive forums, such as Q&A forums for teams to post questions & notify teams
- Set up internal portals that enable sharing of info about changes and encourage open discussions

Virtual meetings
- Encourage regular virtual face-to-face meetings to build camaraderie
- Conduct regular check-ins to gauge progress & issues

Implement comms platforms
- Establish web-based and cloud-based comms platforms
- Define remote comms policies and rules, private & shared message boards & groups

Foster open communications
- Encourage knowledge sharing and build SME capabilities
- Facilitate collaborative work that promotes diversity & varied work experiences

Project management tools

Use project management tools
- Keep track of team assignments, deadlines & workloads using various PM tools / platforms

Customer Experience
- Build enterprise data to enhance CX

Track assignments using statistical reports
- Track and measure team performance using statistical reports that track RAG status, budget

The right digital platform
- Spend time in choosing the right cloud platform

Set clear performance measures (KPIs)
- Set measurable performance goals (KPIs) & how these align with strategic plans

Continuous improvement
- Employ kaizen for continuous improvement

03 The role of a transformation PMO

A transformation PMO is an enterprise department in charge of leading complex organisational strategic initiatives. The PMO serves as a vital link between the executive vision and the company's work. The most important function of a Transformation PMO is to assist the organisation in accomplishing its goals. It's more than just a resource provider; it's also a hub for collaboration, execution, and delivery.

The transformation PMO succeeds when it has the capabilities, processes, and technology to deliver on the CIO's agenda, and then shows measurable business results, such as cost savings, IT stability, and so on. A transformation PMO can manage an organization's whole project and programme portfolio. It is in charge of the organisational pipeline as well as any revisions to the Strategic Roadmap. This comprises enabling, analysing, prioritising, and optimising the project portfolio throughout the Enterprise while balancing strategic goals and trade-offs.

A transformation PMO is in charge of putting an enterprise strategy into action. A PMO connects the strategy to the day-to-day activity, resulting in improved alignment and communication across lines of business and stakeholders. It manages resources and tools to ensure efficient delivery at scale. It keeps track of progress toward goals and provides a comprehensive picture of portfolio health. Finally, a Transformation PMO helps firms attain their full potential by enabling better decision-making through timely and accurate reporting of progress toward targets.

A transformation PMO will ensure that the organisation makes progress by employing proven project management practices. An experienced Transformation PMO will collaborate closely with the initiative's executive sponsor to guarantee that personnel and other necessary resources are available to execute the project on time. A good transformation PMO is integrated with the business's day-to-day operations so that it can overcome line-of-business management resistance and keep an initiative going forward despite obstacles.

IT IS THE MARK OF AN EDUCATED
MIND TO BE ABLE TO ENTERTAIN A
THOUGHT WITHOUT ACCEPTING IT.

Aristotle

The Role a Transformation PMO

Transformation types	Operational	Core transformation	strategic
	Making changes to make operations better, faster, cheaper	Moving to a fundamentally different way of operating	Changing the very essence of the company to a new focus.

Transformation views

Digital	New operating model	New products	New channels	Partnerships	Going multinational

Transformation PMO key functions

Reporting	Technology	Performance monitoring	Competency development	Program promotion
Status Reporting	Implement methodology	Monitor program performance	Develop competencies	Promotion within the firm

Knowledge mgt.	Senior management	Project coordination	Program scoreboard	PMO Performance
Knowledge hub	Senior management advice	Program projects coordination	Develop program scoreboard	Monitor PMO performance

PMO establishment

Goal: PMO established, PMO & program charters, PMO & program policies and governance

Program assessment	PMO Structure	PMO & program facilities	PMO & program governance
Analyse people and processes / Evaluate capabilities	Establish PMO structure / Involve stakeholders	Define PMO & program team needs / Manage PMO & programs	Create PMO & program charter / Create governance

Stakeholder management

Goal: Create stakeholder map & stakeholder management plan

Stakeholder value management	Stakeholder information management	Stakeholder management plan and map
Build stakeholder alliances based on value	Use tool to manage stakeholders & their needs	Create stakeholder management plan

Vendor management

Goal: Agree vendor contracts, deliverables, tracking matrix and communication plan

Vendor management guidelines	Vendor deliverables	Vendor communication guidelines
Develop vendor management guidelines for clarity of goals and requirements	Verify penalties if deliverables & quality are not done. Track deliverables status progress	Set expectations & standards for vendors / Promote vendor guidelines to PM's & vendors

Communications management

Goal: Communication Management. Plan

Communication channels	Stakeholder audience communications
Monitor, control & continuous improvement of comms channels	Understand stakeholder expectations & comms preference

PMO management

Goal: Define PMO governance model, program status report

PMO governance	Program monitoring and control	Program support and reporting
Implement Governance	Ensure the program is under control	Program support including resource needs and program reporting

Knowledge management

Knowledge management hub definition	Knowledge management tool
Design the knowledge management hub	Determine the knowledge management tool needed & implement

04 The digital workplace

Creating a genuinely integrated ecosystem of cutting-edge technologies, platforms, and best practices to digitize the workplace. Achieved in phases and adjustable over time to provide a quick return on investment and long-term competitive advantage. Designed to help enterprises accelerate their digital business transitions by providing faster time to value, integrated functionality, and pre-built components that address common business process concerns. Employee needs and the demands of an increasingly digital world are driving a profound restructuring of workplaces today. People may now work when, where, and how they choose thanks to new tools and technologies. However, for this change to be effective, it must be guided by a compelling vision that relates technology to how people work and interact with one another.

The Digital Workplace is an integrated IT approach that promotes digital dexterity among employees by bringing together the tools, places, workstyles, culture, and skills they require to accomplish their best work and better serve their customers.

The digital workplace is about giving employees a strong new tool to help them do their best work and serve their customers better. It's an integrated IT strategy that promotes digital dexterity among employees and handles some of the most pressing issues they confront in today's workplace. The Digital Workplace supports rich, individualized collaboration, keeping employees informed and engaged at all times.

The Digital Workplace enables employees to reduce their time-to-market securely and efficiently by leveraging market data and insights to adjust plans, processes, and resource allocation; connect with key stakeholders and customers; leverage emerging technologies; and drive business transformation to increase productivity.

ONLY THE DEAD HAVE SEEN THE
END OF WAR.

Plato

The digital workplace

Key digital workplace Q&A

Business goals	Desired results	User needs	Solution vision	Technology
What's the digital transformation targets?	What are the desired digital outcomes?	Who are the users & their needs?	What is the solution vision?	What are the platforms and tools?
Key stakeholders — Whose input required for strategy?	**Stakeholder research** — Capture each stakeholder's plans/ goals	**Research data analysis** — What are the patterns & problems?	**Guiding principles** — What's the strategy guiding principles?	**Strategy feedback** — What's review/ feedback process?
Work environment — Why is there a need to overhaul environment?	**Digital workplace goals** — What is the digital workplace purpose, objectives and goals?	**Employee engagement** — How to exploit tech to raise staff engagement?	**Creativity & collaboration** — How to improve creativity /collaboration?	**Tech tools** — What tech tools does each business function need?
Digital metrics — What could be the metrics for a digital scorecard?	**Changes required** — What changes to internal processes, org. structures, incentives, skills, culture?	**Business processes** — How will these digital workplace efforts change business processes?	**Training** — What training is required for teaching new skills for new digital workplace?	**Digital platforms** — Tie all the digital platforms in a standard architecture to serve customers better
Vision goals — How to increase staff buy in & productivity?	**Roadmap & blueprint** — Establish a roadmap & blueprint to capture initiatives	**Digital metrics** — Create a digital scorecard using analytics to calculate IT, HR & business metrics		**Information** — How to give employees the information they need in the format they need

Why a digital workplace?

Technology framework	Holistic set of platforms	Access data, anyplace, anytime	Productivity & collaboration
An integrated technology framework designed to deliver apps and data	An holistic set of platforms, tools & environments for work delivered in a usable, coherent way	It allows employees to access their apps and data real-time on any device, from any location	It focuses on the experience of the employee to improve productivity & collaboration

The benefits of a digital workplace

Increased efficiency	Decreased costs	Improved customer service
Streamlining operations, digital work places help to operate at peak capacity	Digital workplaces saves money & time and make staff education and training more efficient	Digital workplaces embrace essential techniques like collaboration, analytics, self-service education, and legacy and mobile apps, all of which make it easier to provide outstanding services to customers
Customer interactions — A digital workplace can be very good for increased customer interaction	**Employee engagement** — One of the biggest perks of a digital workplace is increased employee engagement & collaboration	**Breaks down company silos** — It delivers all the tools employees need to accomplish their tasks, while opening up silos
		Collects valuable data — It is also an inherent collector of data this collected data to deliver actionable insights

Emerging digital workplace roles

Digital workplace director	Digital workplace leader	Head of workplace solutions & data
A role to accelerate the technology function to meet business goals, maximise business value from IT investments, and unleash innovation for the organization	A digital workplace leader is an IT leader that works with multidisciplinary talent teams and has deep insight into workplace apps, content services, social networks and technology support	A role to drive strategy & execution for digital measurement capabilities for a well thought out set of measurements that help to drive customer experience & employee productivity

05 OCM & business transformation

Firms must organize change in today's competitive marketplaces to decrease costs and boost revenue. Some businesses excel at innovation, strategic institutionalization, and thinking big while spending modestly. Change is a reaction to external stimuli in which daily actions are modified to attain desired outcomes. To accomplish the intended effects, transformation entails changing underlying beliefs and long-term behaviours, sometimes in significant ways.

The systematic approach and methods you put in place to handle the people-side of change are known as organizational change management in business transformation. Organizational change management is considerably more concerned with the future state and the development of a stronger company or organization. Any shift, realignment, or fundamental change in how a firm runs can be classified as business transformation.

The goal is to make changes to processes, people, or systems (technology) to better align the company with its business strategy and vision for making changes to the way an organization does things to improve, speed up, or reduce costs. Digital transformation is broadly characterized as the use of digital technology to alter services or businesses, but it is more about rethinking how organizations perform and give value to customers than it is about technology. It combines people, processes, and technology, altering old business models to take advantage of the limitless opportunities that digitalization provides.

The concept of digital transformation is supported by three fundamental pillars: getting used to new technology, making decisions based on data and organizational perspectives are being shifted.

THE BEST CURE FOR THE BODY
IS A QUIET MIND.

Napoleon Bonaparte

OCM & business transformation

	Discover	Design	Determine	Deploy
The four stages of change	**Discover** — Introduce change and direction to stakeholders. Create the climate & desire to change. Review the (ASIS) state and launch the Change Network	**Design** — Build understanding of the changes, including support and commitment to those changes. Capture changes to understand the (TOBE) state, & cultural & people impact	**Determine** — Assess progress and ability for workforce to do their jobs in the future (TOBE) state. Address expected changes. Ensure stakeholder preparation and readiness. Establish Helpdesk Go-Live & training focused on support to culture/people	**Deploy** — Encourage and promote adoption, ownership and responsibility for the new (TOBE) end-state. Provide refresher training and comms updates. Transform there business into a service performance-based organization
Five key process steps	**Define the change** — Define the change & align to business goals. Define the what, why, when, who, how (WIIFM). Build awareness and readiness	**Understand the change** — Perform change impact assessment, stakeholder analysis to determine (ASIS) of stakeholders & where they need to be by go live (TOBE)	**Plan for the change** — Develop OCM & stakeholder comms & engagement plans (training planning and audience analysis) / **Action change** — Conduct comms & training tasks. Track progress. and adjust	**Manage & monitor the change** — Monitor stakeholder progress along the change journey. Ensure stakeholders have received the training and support they need to begin feeling comfortable operating under the new (TOBE) state

Three key successful change steps

Change champion network	Change communications	Change training and support
Establish and launch change network. Multi change roles to adopt changes & support stakeholders through changes. change agents drive the change locally change leaders own change plan	'Just Enough, Just in Time' Communications. Determine the audiences (stakeholders). Plan and execute appropriate messages. Communicate what is happening, why, to whom, when and how it will impact. Leverage multiple comms channels	'Just Enough, Just in Time' Training. Deliver training that will provide stakeholders with the required skills and knowledge for the TOBE state. Facilitate a formal 'Day in the Life', end-to end process and system testing for digital transformations & evaluate training

Key change activities - Patterson Connor model

Inform phase	Educate and collaboration phase	Commit phase
Overview (WIIFM): What, Why, Who, When. Introductory deck. Message from Leadership. Project site launch. Internal awareness FAQs and factsheets. Develop & launch the Change Champion Network	Expand project site materials (informational packages, infographics, messages, etc.). Transition to ops & process change reviews. SME workshop sessions. International understanding campaigns. Change network communications	Internal adoption campaigns. Information transition packages / training / simulations for digital transformations. Go-Live readiness workshops. Countdown and go-live comms. Change discussions. Change tracking. Evaluation surveys. Lessons learned

Key change questions

Contact / Acceptance	Awareness / Adoption	Understanding / Ownership	Collaboration / Establishment
Contact — What is this all about?, Why are we doing this? When to happen? / **Acceptance** — What other training and support programs are available?	**Awareness** — How will this change impact me and my job? Where can I find info on the change initiative? / **Adoption** — Can we receive extra training and support in completing tasks under the new (TOBE) state?	**Understanding** — How can I help? What are the risks associated with this change? / **Ownership** — How can I help others use the new (TOBE) state?, How to improve?"	**Collaboration** — How will my performance measures change? How can I participate in and promote the migration to the new (TOBE) state? / **Establishment** — How can we share our success stories? How can we sustain this change? Can this change be applied to other areas?

OCM lessons learned

Early change management planning	Change impact assessments	Change tools and measures	Training & support
Ensure early OCM planning during the current (ASIS) state to prepare culture and people for change and create climate for change. Include comms and training	Ensure key changes by function & process areas are documented for future state (TOBE). Ensure all stakeholder groups are identified, including leadership	Ensure proper change tools are in place for effective adoption and sustainment. Measure for success. Use qualitative & quantitative KPIs	Train stakeholders. Evaluate change success. Provide refresher training

06 The 5 stages of digital maturity

In these modern times, a fresh approach to digitalization is becoming increasingly required. Organizations are at various stages of readiness or maturity to deal with all of the activities that develop as a result of such a significant strategy shift as digital transformation.

Digital transformation is more than just a new technology or a new method of working. It necessitates a disruptive and strategic strategy, as well as a disruptive and transformative approach. Most firms' strategies to compete in the digital age now include digital transformation. Almost every organization recognizes that this is a key issue for survival, yet many are having difficulty getting started, or if they do get started, they quickly become stuck.

Despite increasing investments in digital projects, many businesses are unable to see a return on their investment. Organizations benefit greatly from digital transformation, yet more than three-quarters of businesses are still in the early phases of this journey.

According to research, many businesses are at various stages of readiness or maturity to deal with all of the activities that result from such a significant strategy shift, and there are five stages of digital maturity (digital readiness). The five stages of digital maturity provides a framework for determining where a business is on its digital transformation journey so that action may be taken to move forward.

NEVER SPEND YOUR MONEY
BEFORE YOU HAVE IT.

Thomas Jefferson

The 5 stages of digital maturity

DT maturity	Strengths, opportunities and gaps	Business challenges	Create a plan
	Identify strengths & opportunities and gaps for digital	Address the business challenges	Create an digital action plan to fix issues
Maturity levels	Organizations are at different levels of maturity to tackle all the initiatives that arise from such a strategic change that comes with Transformation		
Stage 1: siloed	Stage 1: At this stage, Organizations have a strong silo-view of separate competing business units where IT is just a support function		
Stage 2: isolated	Stage 2: Some business units starts realising some business benefits of transformation but isolated in terms of the bigger business picture		
Stage 3: sync	Stage 3: Coordinated programs for strategic transformation across the enterprise		
State 4: strategic	Stage 4: Completed digital platforms, products and processes for digital transformation		
Stage 5: agile	Stage 5: This final stage is when digital & non-digital practices for an agile business that can respond rapidly to any changes in market conditions		

Governance & leadership	Governance & Leadership is creating the right environment & culture for successful collaboration, innovation, and execution		
	Balance strong oversight	**Clearly define accountabilities**	**Define measures of success**
	Set strategic direction centrally, but units work together to deliver digital platforms	Set clear responsibilities across key decision areas to support platform autonomy, transparency & efficiency	Define measures for the success of the strategy against goals, user experience, business benefits

Organization	Organization is the culture, customer focus, innovation, risk appetite, and attention to change. Digitization transforms organizations on 3 levels		
	External focus	**Internal focus**	**Holistic focus**
	The external focus is on the customer experience and external comms of the firm	The internal focus is on the operations, internal comms & decision making of the firm	The digital strategy must be holistic & inclusive of all business functions

Culture and innovation	Culture & Innovation is the will & the capacity to evaluate & implement new technologies & business processes		
	Encourages outward looking	**Match digital strategy to culture**	**Change is difficult – pick your battles**
	A digital culture encourages employees to look outward and engage with customers & partners to develop new solutions	Senior management should Focus away from strategy and instead prioritise the cultural alignment of the transformation	Focus on a few critical (and achievable) behaviour changes like focus on getting small functional teams like shadow each other

Technology	Digital transformation can involve many technologies but the hottest topics right now are cloud computing, the Internet of Things, big data, and AI	
	Successful DT is not just technology	**Use technology to transform processes, products and services**
	DT is not just about tech. Changing core processes & culture are vital to DT success	Transform existing processes to become more efficient by using technology not just to replicate existing services in a digital form, but to transform these services into something better

Capabilities & abilities							
Flexible, secure infrastructure	Data mastery	Digital savvy talent	Ecosystem engagement	Intelligent workflows	Unified CX	Business adaptability

07 Successful transformation

Traditionally, business transformation programmes have focused on increasing productivity by taking a "better, faster, and cheaper" approach to how a company operates. Leaders may improve productivity, accountability, transparency, execution, and decision-making speed by adopting a disciplined approach.

Clear program ownership, high-quality connections throughout the transformation team, and an awareness of the business environment are the characteristics that define the most effective transformations. These individuals have clear ownership of their projects, collaborate well with their peers heading other initiatives, and appreciate the importance of their specific work within the overall transformation effort in the most successful transformations.

Leaders must be exceptionally skilled at developing high-performing transformation teams if they are to accomplish results at the scale and speed that enterprises today demand. Combining a highly trained team of internal subject matter experts with specialist resources to give the necessary assistance results in the most effective company transformations.

When these groups cooperate and make choices together, they will be able to make real-time course adjustments and accelerate the transition.

THE SECRET OF GETTING AHEAD
IS GETTING STARTED.

Mark Twain

Successful transformation

Plans failure	**Inefficient execution** Underestimating the amount of effort that is required for a true transformation	**Lack of agility** A plan is important but a plan with no flexibility will fail. It is not possible to see all the unforeseen challenges and risks so not having long term detailed plans upfront is a recipe for failure	**Wrong plan balance** Having wrong balance in plans, agility projects, quick wins, timeline, budget & resources	**Budget constraints** Not understanding the full cost (resources, processes, systems) to achieve the result	**Resilience** Mistakes will happen & leaders to be resilient
Leadership failure	**Lack of commitment** Lack of leadership commitment to see the transformation through to the end to deliver the required business results	**No vision for change** If the Organization has a leader who does not see the need for a major change, the transformation is doomed to failure	**Manager paralysis** Without strong leadership it will be be difficult to move managers from their risk averse roles to change	**One vision, one goal** Transformation depends on everyone being aligned and moving towards the same goal	**Dishonesty** If leaders are not honest about the present, this can be a driver for failure
Approach failure	**Using waterfall only** Using waterfall approach instead of an iterative/ hybrid waterfall approach is a common BT failure	**Traditional PMO's** It is beyond most PMOs' capability to execute & achieve successful change in a transformation	**Too focused on now** Transformation focused on present issues may miss the transformation & innovation for 2 to 5 years	**Things are too good** If a company is doing well already, it is hard to promote change for the better from the status quo	**Lack of PPM** No project prioritization result in resource issues
Process failure	**Skipping discovery** Lack of thorough analysis of the ASIS— cost, time, data, workflow, cycle time, customer needs often leads to failed TOBE implementation	**Focus on technology** Most transformations focus more on the technical solution than on the processes around the solution, including pain areas, broken processes, and delay	**No WIIFM** Failure to establish the "What's In It For Me", what is happening, why, to whom, when, & how it will impact processes and systems leads to disengaged staff	**Poor 'TOBE' design** Poor TOBE state design and documentation, including future roles (RACIs), KPIs, system interactions, channels, inputs, outputs, and improvements	**Enterprise process** A lack of enterprise-wide business process to implement the transformation strategy.
Change failure	**Comms & training** Lack of (early and continuous) comms and proper training at all levels of the firm	**Change network** No change network to support change. Change agent who drive the change locally and change leaders, who own the change	**Too much too soon** Doing a big bang transformation approach can overwhelm staff especially if they have not been properly prepared for the change	**Too much all the time** Transformation failure exhaustion, the resulting fatigue that happens due to continuous change	**Focus on journey** Firms are often stuck on textbook change methods without adapting to own needs and change journey
Execution failure	**Wrong mix in team** Getting the balance wrong with the right mix of internal staff and external vendors and consultants	**Unforeseen challenges** Lack of long-term detailed plans up front for unforeseen challenges & risks is a recipe for failure	**Implementation time** A long implementation time without prioritized efforts based on quick wins/ visible results demotivates staff	**Small things hurt** Transformation failures can occur from small cuts, so effective comms and change management is key	**Infrastructure** Not having a process to align the infrastructure to support the transformation

08 Integrated workstreams for BT

A business transformation is more than just a destination; it's a journey. Infrastructure, organisation, and procedures all require successful transformation and management. To help organisations meet their overall objectives, the integrated workstreams for business transformation solution addresses those aspects of transformation in the areas of Business Process Re-engineering (BPR), Organizational Change Management (OCM), Project and Portfolio Management, and organisational design.

To fully enjoy the benefits of a transformation implementation, processes, behaviours, and culture must adapt. However, many transformation implementations continue via sequential change activities with little effort to combine them into a cohesive implementation.

Integrating workstreams (e.g., organisational and change management, business process re-engineering, systems integration, and so on) is a critical success element when it comes to conducting business transformations to increase overall performance and control. Business transformation necessitates the execution of numerous interconnected workstreams, but their integration is frequently overlooked. Implementation leaders are faced with the task of meeting aggressive objectives and timelines while also managing interdependencies to finish their change efforts successfully. BPR, OCM, organisational design, enterprise project management, and process automation are all key activities for coordinating and integrating numerous workstreams.

Successful business transformations use an integrated workstreams approach to ensure that key change elements like BPR, OCM, organisational design, and enterprise project management are all taken into account holistically to ensure a successful implementation and maximise the value of a transformation programme.

THERE'S A MILLION THINGS I
HAVEN'T DONE, BUT JUST YOU
WAIT. JUST YOU WAIT.

Alexander Hamilton

Integrated workstreams for BT

Organizational design

	Develop project charter	Develop strategy	Assessment	Design
	Establish Project Charter Conduct summary ASIS analysis	Review external environment Assess ASIS strategy and goals	Analyse processes &structure Review culture	Establish design guidelines & principles Define business model
	Design alternative TOBE organization models Educate leaders & assign design team	Create TOBE vision, strategy project scorecard	Benchmark similar organizations Report to steering team	Redesign processes & structure Verify the design

	Transition	Implement	Evaluate
	Assign implementation team	Reconfigure systems / locations	Assess performance vs. scorecard
	Create execution plans	Implement new org. structures,	Make adjustments to design
	Train people in new roles	Monitor progress	

Change management

- **Define change & establish the change network:** Define what needs to change and why, then align to the strategy & goals
- **Training for desired skills & behaviours:** Communicate the change & provide training to business results
- **Determine the impacts:** Determine change impacts, who & how impacted
- **Decide best support for transition:** Decide where support is required for a smooth transition
- **Communication strategy:** Develop a comms strategy to communicate & monitor feedback
- **Measure change progress & evaluate:** Assess if the CM process was successful to achieve the goals

Business process reengineering

- **Define business processes:** Map the ASIS state (activities, workflows, rules, roles, relationships, technology)
- **Design TOBE processes:** Use the improvements (time and cost based) with most impact on form effectiveness, efficiency aligned to strategic aims
- **Analyse business processes:** Identify gaps & causes for improving Organizational effectiveness, efficiency & strategic goal alignment
- **Operationalize TOBE changes:** Ensure new (TOBE) processes are embedded, communicated users trained on the new processes before implementation
- **Identify improvement opportunities:** Identify & validate opportunities to act on the analysis results including identifying transformation opportunities
- **Changes with linkages to other workstreams:** Link TOBE implementation to other work streams: OD, change management, enterprise performance management & agile PMO

Enterprise performance management

- **Strategy development & translation:** Strategy development determines an organization direction for strategy: mission, vision, strategic goals, Strategy translation translates the strategy into particular organization actions with KPIs
- **Business planning:** Business planning & forecasting is a set of business activities planned against the strategy with forecasted results in a specific time period
- **Financial management:** Financial management refers to the set business processes done to close the financial records of a format the end of a period timely and accurate
- **Supply chain effectiveness:** Supply Chain Effectiveness is the capabilities to manage an enterprise supply chain but also provide transparency to all parts of the value chain

Agile PMO

- **Agile project management:** Initiate, plan and execute agile process groups, especially those that can be employed in multiple domains (eg. scrum)
- **Project standards and quality:** Ensure PM standards & quality for high project maturity, a factor for project success
- **Agile program management:** Provide a centralized view of status & metrics for all projects & for program as a whole. Resource mgmt. & load-balancing across projects
- **Project effectiveness and efficiency:** Agile PMO can improve efficiency and effectiveness by promoting the same PM standards and processes
- **Agile portfolio management:** Optimize ROI by analyzing proposed and current projects & programs. Value "responding to change over following a plan"
- **Continuous improvement:** The continuous improvement of agile PM is a factor for an org undergoing transformation

09 Digital transformation strategy

For many firms, digital transformation has become a top priority. A digital transformation strategy accelerates the process of digitizing all aspects of your business, including processes, products, and business models, to better fulfil customer expectations and achieve a competitive advantage. For businesses seeking to stay up with digital disruption, digital transformation represents a significant shift.

Effective analysis and vision, devoted leadership, cross-functional collaboration, and a diversity of people managing initiatives are all essential components of a successful digital transformation plan. A good digital transformation strategy examines a company's culture, establishes business objectives, recognizes and documents risks, conducts periodic pilots and testing, and solicits employee feedback on the implementations. Companies must build an internal network of innovators and early adopters that can generate good first customer reviews to proceed with new technologies on a larger scale.

Analysing organizational culture, creating business goals, identifying and documenting new technology risks, assessing progress often, and asking for feedback during rollout should all be part of a digital transformation strategy. Digital transformations are commonly used by businesses to improve business processes. The thoughts of company executives and employees should be incorporated into a digital transformation strategy.

To ensure that the plan is inclusive across the organization, leaders need to make sure to include all key stakeholders from various departments. Also organizations should avoid making the usual error of making the digital transformation a technology-driven endeavour by focusing on the company's customers' demands and business goals.

SIMPLICITY IS THE ULTIMATE
SOPHISTICATION.

Leonardo da Vinci

Digital transformation strategy

Key questions

Current state — Where are the current company problems?

Best in class — What does the business do best in class?

Desired state — Where does the business want to be in the market?

The direction — Where is the organization headed?

Policies — What policies to define to get organization to the "TO BE" state?

Metrics — How to measure strategy success?

Growth and financial objectives — What are the growth and financial objectives?

Leadership — Is there leadership commitment for the strategy?

Customers — How to bring customers closer to the business?

Growth — How to Identify opportunities for growth & innovation?

Opportunities — What are the opportunities for business now & future?

Markets — What's the customers buying habits & behaviors?

Events — What are the political, economic, social and technological events that could impact the business?

Opportunities — How best to leverage new market opportunities?

Business objectives

Financials — To increase earnings

Market share — Increase market share

Customer perception — To improve customer perception

Operation costs — To attain lower operational costs

Products — Lead in products & services

Technology superiority — Achieve superiority using innovation

Situation analysis

Internal organizational factors
- What is the organization's internal situation?
- What are business strengths and weaknesses?
- What are the capability gaps in the organization?

Technology platforms — What are the right technology platforms / development methodologies / security mechanisms to deliver digital business scale, speed & flexibility?

Marketing — What is the most effective marketing activities?

Operational processes — How to transform operational processes to keep pace with the change of customer needs and behaviors?

Employee experience — How to attract and retain talent within organization?

Data driven marketing
- How to improve data driven decision making?
- Does data support the business strategic needs?

Workflows — How to build strategic business process workflows that are automated, intelligent and efficient?

Existing programs and projects — Are existing initiatives being reviewed for alignment with strategic objectives and if not, stopped?

Externa; factors
- What are the opportunities
- What are the threats?
- What are the competitive moves of rivals?
- What are the success factors?

Architectures — Is the business architecture aligned with the technology / security architecture?

Continuous improvement — How to foster a culture of continuous improvement?

Competitive analysis

Competition
- What are the competitors doing?
- Who uses identical technological approaches?

Digital competitors — What is the best approach and activities on how to take on digital competitors?

Competitor strategies
- What are the current strategies of competitors?
- What are the strengths and weaknesses of each competitor?

Competitive advantage — How to create competitive advantages and deliver them in the form of technology solutions that increases efficiency and brings the customer closer to the business?

10 EA in digital transformation

Enterprise architecture (EA) is the process of directing enterprise IT systems toward value-driven business outcomes. In recent years, the role of enterprise architects has become increasingly critical at the leadership table. An EA programme that is well-managed can help a company stay competitive, be more efficient, and help with digital transformation.

The role of the enterprise architecture (EA) team has become so critical to digital transformation that it cannot be overlooked. As the digital space is evolving at a rapid pace, EA teams are faced with plenty of challenges. For large companies, the enterprise architecture (EA) department can play a central role in reducing the complexity associated with digital transformations. Enterprise architecture connects these complex technologies with business context to drive desirable business outcomes.

Enterprise Architecture creates a common language for both business and IT departments to use, enabling better collaboration across the enterprise on digital initiatives. Enterprise architecture (EA) is a practice that aims to create strategic alignment, unify and streamline operations by defining business processes, information flows, and governance models.

EA provides the guidelines to allow organizations to leverage existing assets in new ways and make adjustments when needed. In this course, you will learn how different EA functions accelerate the pace of digital transformation through strong governance, increased agility and improved operational excellence.

**HAPPINESS AND MORAL DUTY
ARE INSEPARABLY CONNECTED.**

George Washington

EA in digital transformation

Digital transformation	**Digital transformation** Digital transformation is the transformation of business and firm activities, processes, & business models to fully leverage the changes and opportunities of digital technologies	**DT creates challenges across the firm** Digital transformation imposes areas of advancement in the form of challenges for an organization. These new developments pushes a company to be more agile, customer-centric, innovative, efficient, and team-oriented	**DT creates challenges to systems** Becoming an agile company, rapidly iterating new applications holds the key to digital transformation success. Unfortunately, many firms have applications & IT architectures that pose significant challenges to rapid iteration
Digital strategy, transformation and architecture	**Digital strategy** An firm's digital positioning, operating model, customers & partners	**Digital architecture** The "TOBE" state for applications, data and technologies to achieve digital operating status	**Business process extension** The extending and exposing of an organization's business processes outside the company
A digital strategy	**A digital strategy** • Why a firm needs a digital strategy? • What gives rise to the need for it? • What problems trying to solve? • What challenges to address? • What constraints looking to remove?	**The core objectives of a digital strategy** • What are its objectives? • What is the long-term digital strategy? • How to communicate the results of the goals? • How to measure the results of the goals? • How will the implementation be phased?	**The action plan for a digital strategy** • What is the schedule for implementation? • What are the technology & system pre-requisite? What are the resource & organization pre-requisites for success? • What are the risks and dependencies? • How to create a realistic and achievable plan?
Technology challenges with EA role and digital transformation	**Greater complexity with systems** Businesses experience greater complexity in systems & processes as digital projects are rolled out and with expansion of DT enterprise programs	**IT may need to do a lot of reengineering** IT organizations may need significant systems & applications reengineering to enable basic digital activities & firms may be slowed down to market with new products & services	**EA has rules &processes around technology** EA responsible of entire systems architecture, business processes & IT infrastructure. It makes rules for processes for technology usage to ensure consistency across business units
The impact of having no enterprise architecture or digital transformation	**Reduced flexibility** Organizations are unable to exploit economies of scale without an enterprise architecture in place	**Increased organizational costs** Organizations suffer from increased costs from duplication of resources to develop, operate & maintain business systems	**Increased delays in delivering changes** Technology complexity causes difficulties with changes to underlying processes, applications, systems & infrastructure
The benefits of EA involvement in digital transformation	**Improved documentation** When EA is involved in DT projects, the documentation and communication between business and IT stakeholders improves significantly	**More focus on tangible DT benefits** Companies can focus on capturing tangible benefits from digital transformation by reducing technology risks using EA & have more focus on planning given the reduced complexity	**Benefits can only come form EA involvement** EA groups can suffer from lack of visibility in companies & senor leaders need to raise the profile of EA to develop the business & interpersonal capabilities of their EA architects
The value of an effective enterprise architecture	**EA promotes effective IT** EA rules and policies promote a more efficient and effective IT Infrastructure	**Improved IT and business alignment** Improved alignment IT investment plans with planned business initiatives, priorities and requirements	**EA facilitates info sharing** Having an enterprise architecture promotes & facilitates cross-organizational sharing of enterprise data & information
	Responsive IT to business requirements IT can be more responsive to business needs with an integrated enterprise architecture	**Raises visibility of best practices** An effective enterprise architecture raises the visibility of innovations and best practices across the business enterprise	**EA rules ensure traceability of decisions** EA rules and a an enterprise architecture ensures the traceability of decisions by functions

11 Disruptive innovation

Disruptive innovations are unanticipated product and service innovations that offer lower prices and acceptable performance than incumbent products and services. It's a product or service that either disrupts an existing market or develops an entirely new one. In practise, disruption occurs when typical market value drivers are drastically altered.

It's a breakthrough that makes products and services more accessible to untapped or underserved populations by simplifying them and making them more inexpensive. Established businesses tend to focus on improving their products and services for their profitable customer base, while mainly disregarding the requirements and desires of new markets. When the mainstream market abandons old items in favour of new products, disruption occurs.

Artificial intelligence, blockchain, 3D printing, VR/AR, and IoT are the most recent disruptive technologies. E-commerce, online news sites, ride-sharing apps, and GPS systems are examples of disruptive technology uses. Automobiles, electricity, and television were disruptive technology in their own time.

Disruptive innovation allows businesses to take a step back and evaluate their current products and services, as well as identify areas where improvements can be made, as well as identify consumer requirements that could benefit from an inventive solution. In the business world, innovation gives you an edge over the competition since disruption gives customers and society new possibilities that other companies haven't been able to deliver.

THE MIND IS NOT A VESSEL
TO BE FILLED BUT A FIRE TO
BE KINDLED.

Plutarch

Disruptive innovation

Disruptive innovation

Disruption is a process
Disruption is a process, not a product or service, that occurs fringe to mainstream

Originates in low end or new markets
Originate in low-end (less demanding customers) or new market (where none existed)

New firms need to match quality
New firms don't catch on with mainstream customers until quality matches their standards

Disruptive business not always successful
Success is not a requirement & some business can be disruptive & fail

A different business model
New firm's business model differs significantly from incumbent

Four stages of disruption

The four stages of disruption described by Steven Sinofsky are disruption, evolution, convergence and re-imagination

Phase one: disruption of incumbent
incumbent's attitudes towards tech disruption range from "new tech is inferior", "new products do not do all the things existing products do" to "new services fail to address existing needs that is already in place

Phase 2: rapid linear evolution
The product creators are still disruptors, innovating along the trajectory they set for themselves, with a strong focus on early-adopter customers. The incumbents continue the ASIS trajectory, sealing their fate

Phase 3: appealing convergence
As the market redefinition proceeds, the category of a new product starts to undergo a subtle redefinition. The market begins to call for the replacement of the incumbent tech with the new technology

Phase 4: complete reimagination
The last stage of technology disruption is when a category or technology is reimagined from the ground up with new criteria such as cost, performance, reliability, service and features

Disruptive services

Disruptive Innovations they make products & services more accessible & affordable

Uber is **not** an example of disruption because it didn't originate in a low-end / a new market

A low-cost solution to a low-value customer. Of course, as **Airbnb** grew in popularity, the quality of its offering increased. They met the needs of high value customers who usually stay in nice hotels

Netflix started off as a video on demand and DVD by mail. Netflix is a disruptive innovation as it revolutionised how people get their daily dose of entertainment

Amazon is one most disruptive firms as users love it so much they forget how much expense

Disruptive technologies

A disruptive technology sweeps away the systems as it has attributes that are recognizably superior

Alexa
The smart speaker is changing the way people interact

Artificial intelligence (AI)
AI emphasizes the creation of intelligent machines that work and react like humans.

Internet of things (IOT)
IoT consists of all the web-enabled devices that collect, send and act on data they acquire using embedded sensors

3D printing
3D printing is a way of creating three dimensional (3D) solid objects. 3D printing is done by building up the object layer by layer.

Robotics
Robotics is a part of Engineering and Science. It is focuses on the creation and building of robots, as well as computer programming

Blockchain
Blockchain is a type of diary of transactions with a separate copy s spread over many computers

The benefits of disruptive innovation

Helps expand markets
It aids businesses to expand its markets through innovation with new & existing products

A sense of urgency
It creates a sense of urgency for businesses to the importance of embracing new tech.

Future leaders
It helps companies discover its present &future leaders who understand what disruptive innovation brings

Future opportunities
Disruptive innovation helps businesses discover future opportunities in the marketplace

Change in culture
A business culture can change into a learning firm that embraces change & innovation

12 AI Applications

Throughout industry and academia, artificial intelligence (AI) has been applied in applications to solve unique challenges. Artificial intelligence, like electricity and computers, is a general-purpose technology with a wide range of uses. The tools and technology that enable computers and machines to do intelligent activities are referred to as Artificial Intelligence Applications. As more corporations build machine learning algorithms for their goods, artificial intelligence (AI) is becoming more common.

Artificial intelligence (AI) applications are software systems and machines that can do jobs that would ordinarily need human intelligence. Visual perception, speech recognition, decision-making, and language translation are examples of such activities. Machine learning is a popular topic of AI research because it allows computers to learn without being explicitly programmed or requiring human input. Algorithms in machine learning create models based on sample data and generate predictions.

The simulation of human intelligence processes by machines, particularly computer systems, is known as artificial intelligence. Expert systems, natural language processing, speech recognition, and machine vision are examples of AI applications. Applications of artificial intelligence (AI), such as autonomous vehicles and medical diagnosis, have enormous potential to change the world. Siri, self-driving cars, robot vacuum cleaners, entertainment, search engines, online assistants, picture recognition, spam filtering, online advertisements, banking, finance, surveillance, education, and space exploration are some of the other AI applications.

Cybersecurity must deal with a variety of cyber assaults that affect all types of businesses. To improve their systems, security organizations have begun to use neural networks, machine learning, and natural language processing (NLP) solutions.

TASTE IS THE COMMON SENSE OF
GENIUS.

Victor Hugo

AI Applications

Industry	Application	Description
Healthcare	Automation of evaluation	Automate initial evaluation of a CT scan / EKG
Healthcare	Identify high risk patients	Identify high-risk patients for population health
Healthcare	Solve costs of wrong dosage	Ai use to determine accurate doses of drugs
Healthcare	Find treatments for cancer	AI helps doctors find right treatments for cancer
Automotive	Self driving cars	The creation and evolution of self-driving vehicles
Automotive	Self driving trucks	The innovation of self-driving trucks is possible
Automotive	Pre-programmed maps	Eliminate the need for pre-programmed maps
Automotive	How handle high risk decisions	How to handle head-on collision with walkers
Finance	Banks use AI for many banking tasks	Banks use AI today to organize operations and invest in stocks
Finance	The use of AI in automated decision making	AI machines used in applications such as online trading & decision making
Cybersecurity	Security companies use AI and natural language processing	Use AI and NLP to automatically sort the data in networks into high risk and low-risk information
Cybersecurity	The use of AI to detect viruses and malware	AI systems are learning to detect viruses & malware by using complex algorithms
Government	AI paired with facial recognition for mass surveillance	Artificial intelligence paired with facial recognition systems may be used for mass surveillance
Government	The use of AI to manage city traffic	AI has been use manage traffic signal systems in a city to normalise the flow of traffic
Law	AI doing tasks that were previously done by entry level lawyers	AI analytics to do work previously done by entry-level lawyers
Law	The use of AI to predict legal outcomes	AI has the ability to tell lawyers their chances of winning relevant cases
Video games	AI used for non-player characters	AI is used to generate dynamic non-player characters (NPCs)
Video games	Use AI to generate new games	AI software working alongside human partners, creates new video games
Military	AI used to enhance communications and sensors	AI used to enhance communications, sensors and Interoperability
Military	AI used for autonomous military robots and drones	AI being used for military drones, robots & unmanned vehicles
Hospitality	AI used to reduce staff load and increase efficiency	AI based solutions are used to reduce staff and increase efficiency
Hospitality	Hotel use AI for virtual assistance robots	Hotel services backed by AI use chatbot application, and service robots
Audit	AI used for continuous audits	AI makes continuous audit with overall audit time and risk reduced
Audit	AI makes it easier for auditors to work better and smarter	AI optimizes their time, to judge and analyse a broader set of data
Advertising	AI predicting customer behaviours to target promotions	AI predicts customer behaviour using digital footprints, to target with personalized promotions
Advertising	The use of AI to reduce the cost of advertising campaigns	Personality computing AI can reduce cost of advertising campaigns by psychological targeting
Art	AI used to create visual art	AI has inspired creative applications to produce visual art
Art	AI is really good at creating poetry	AI is so good at poetry that humans think they were created by a person
Voice assistants	Siri is a popular voice assistant used in Apple products	Siri uses machine-learning technology to be capable-to-understand natural language requests
Voice assistants	Amazon's voice assistant Alexa used over 100M devices	Amazon says Alexa can now guess what you might be thinking of, or what you've forgotten

13 Key factors for transformation

Digitalization is using digital technologies to change business models. It can give organizations a competitive advantage by doing things better, faster, and cheaper than the competition. The key factors of digital transformation include structures, processes, people, technologies and knowledge. Digitalization is reshaping all industries. Use innovative internet-based business models through digitalization.

Digital technologies are now so pervasive that many organizations have found themselves having to fundamentally rethink the way they do business. Digitalization is using digital technologies to change business models. Digitalization enables new business models and changing customer behaviour, by changing the way we work and interact with information. In turn, it unlocks innovation, new services and increased efficiencies.

Digital technologies-cloud, mobile, big data and analytics-are driving digital transformation. Data analytics is a focal point of digitalization. There is an abundance of data available on stakeholders (customers, suppliers, competitors, employees), products (e.g., sales, shipments), services (e.g., service calls, complaints), and finances (e.g. costs, supply chain risks).

Organizations want to become digital leaders by focusing on the customer experience and anticipating their needs. Digital technologies are used by companies to enhance customer experiences and make internal business operations more effective and efficient. There are three essential components of a digital transformation: the overhaul of processes, the overhaul of operations, and the overhaul of relationships with customers.

IF I HAVE SEEN FARTHER THAN OTHERS,
IT IS BECAUSE I WAS STANDING ON THE
SHOULDERS OF GIANTS.

Isaac Newton

Key factors for transformation

Customer understanding

Know your customers
Knowing your customers is data collected by a business so they know who their customers are, what they buy and use etc. Understanding them helps to deliver products with compelling value propositions

Understand your customers
Understanding your customer is about knowing what they want, what their needs are, and how their needs change & delivering that customer experience in the best method available

Customer touchpoints

Social media	Reviews and ratings	Testimonials	Word of mouth	Advertising	Marketing and PR
Retail store	Website	Promotions	Sales team	points of sale	Phone system
Billing	Emails & texts	Marketing emails	Support teams	Online help centre	Service teams

Sales proposition

1. Audience — Identify target audience
2. Problem — Explain problem to solve
3. Biggest benefits — List biggest product benefits
4. Sales promise — What is your customer promise?
5. Refine — Combine steps 1-4 into 1
6. Condense paragraph — Cut down words to a sentence

Performance management

Performance management
Performance management is the process of creating a work environment or setting in which people are enabled to perform to the best of their abilities

Performance management tools
Alongside KPIs, performance appraisals are probably the most commonly used performance management tool aligning the goals of individuals with the strategic aims of the organization

Automation

Fixed automation
It is a system in which the sequence of processing operations is fixed by the equipment configuration

Programmable automation
This system is designed with the capability to change the sequence of operations for different product configurations done by a program

Flexible automation
This system is capable of producing a variety of products with virtually no time lost for changeovers of products

Visualizing individual work

1. Use imagery for success — Have staff focus on the process of reaching success & what result feels like
2. Get employees excited — Encourage staff to be positive, find excitement & purpose about projects and their goals
3. Create a visual strategy — Employees need to visualize the goals they should accomplish & then link to the corporate strategy
4. Create vision board — Encourage staff to create a vision board for their dreams & goals for the organization.

Digitizing the business

Set digital protocols
The core of what it takes to digitize is planning. It's key to consider how digitization will impact business processes

Provide mobile support
A critical component of how to digitize your business is mobile support as most people use smartphones, which makes it a must

Incorporate cloud technologies
A business digitization plan often includes a few cloud-based technologies as CRM & Knowledge Management System (KMS)

Partner relationships — Expanding your team with third party digital skills increases digitisation business success
Target customer experience — Digitization of business processes needs staff from all teams for an end-to-end customer experience
Reduce potential bottlenecks — it's a priority to finish business digitization & it's critical to avoid & prevent potential bottlenecks
Review customer feedback — It's vital to evaluate customer feedback at every point of development, from alpha to beta to live

New digital products & services

Digital products
A digital product is any product you can sell virtually. It comes in digital form downloadable from the internet & easier to manage, less expensive to create, and just as easy to market

Digital services
Digital Services are the electronic delivery of information across multiple platforms & devices like web or mobile with benefits of reduced costs, improved efficiency and high levels of customer service.

14 Transformation lessons learned

For more than a decade, companies have been undergoing digital transformation (DX). The use of new digital technology to processes, services, and products that radically alters how businesses operate is known as digital transformation. For some, the DX efforts have resulted in a total overhaul of the customer service, product and service delivery, and operations models. Digital transformation is more than just a technological movement; it is also a cultural shift toward a culture of constant innovation, fast experimentation, and testing. It uproots and replaces existing behaviours and processes with new digital ones. Delivering value necessitates the engagement of multiple business functions.

A digital transformation is a change management and technology approach that enables organizations to realize their full potential by leveraging new digital capabilities. Using mobility, analytics, and social media, this approach involves migrating from legacy technology and corporate processes to cloud computing.

Most businesses will want to hasten their Digital Transformation efforts, but they will fail to fully account for the consequences of change. Because people are often averse to change, well-written business cases that clearly articulate the project's benefits are essential. A common theme in successful Digital Transformation initiatives is that they take a cross-functional approach to the initiative, where the buy-in is not assumed to be optional, and they conduct a thorough analysis of business needs, the impact it will have on employees, customers, partners, and end-users, before focusing on enabling the business.

Two key takeaways are that product, service, and business innovation is a team sport, and that effective changes come from both the bottom and the top.

BE THE CHANGE THAT YOU WISH TO
SEE IN THE WORLD.

Gandhi

Leadership

Strong DT vision
Successful DT leaders communicate a clear vision about DT – what is the plan, why, to whom, when, and how it will be executed

Enterprise-wide strategy
Successful DT projects are enterprise driven and deliver a shared vision & planning, consistency & common data

Use the CEO for DT
Successful DT projects involves people, culture & business models beyond the scope of a CIO and requires the power & budget of a CEO

Enterprise impact
Successful DT projects understand the enterprise impact to people, process, data, process, technology & clients from transformation

`Economies of scale
Taking an enterprise governance approach will achieve economies of scale for improved DT success

Business

Business goals
Successful DT (business & technology driven) DT aligns to business goals & has a valid business case

Customers
Successful DT connects to the needs & requirements of customers & partners

Make DT real
Ensure DT initiative is not just leader's hype & that it is linked to real digital success

Steering committee
Best practice for a steering committee to guide digital efforts & use COE digital team

Centralized units
Successful DT initiatives leverage centralised IT and business units

Business buy-in
Even technology driven DT requires buy-in & engagement from the business

Process

ASIS state discovery
Successful DT initiatives include a review and documentation of ASIS processes, including a summary of the ASIS state

Gap analysis
Successful DT initiatives identify customer requirements, critical process metrics, process and system constraints

TOBE state design
Successful DT initiatives identify and document TOBE processes and confirm the design principles: Simple, Customer-Centric and Lean

TOBE state planning
Successful DT initiatives plan for successful change implementation, building rollout action plans to address expected changes

TOBE state deployment
Successful DT initiatives create ownership of the change, monitor compliance & user adoption, assess stakeholder alignment to DT

Change

People and change
DT is just about the people involved and impacted as it is about the technology and process change. More focus on the people and culture transformation

Assess change impacts
Successful DT invests in change impact assessments, identifies and analyses stakeholder groups & training needs, reviews & validates change impacts

Change communications
Stakeholders need to have an efficient and clear comms process to provide their feedback on any DT projects, plus face-to-face / 1:1 w/ leadership

Manage expectations
Successful leaders expect problems with DT projects, they anticipate the issues and set expectations to stake- holders at start & implementation

Continual change
Successful leaders set expectations that DT is not a one-time project. They focus on long-term improvements and continually challenge the status quo

Projects

Multi-discipline
Successful DT initiatives are multi-discipline, enterprise and business team driven projects

Third parties
Ensure the use of vendors & consultants, their payment incentives are linked to a DT project successful outcome

Agile and iterative projects
Moving to the cloud with migration of data & work is no small step and can have big risks. An agile & iterative approach to managing the DT can optimize and simplify the transformation process

Project communications
When implementing DT initiatives, cross-team project communication is essential to ensure engagement, & collaboration within project members

Digital regulation
Expect more digital regulation in the future from governments so build digital regulation, security compliance and governance into DT plans

Technology

Customer experience
Use DT initiative to build a strong enterprise data foundation to enhance the customer experience

Manage hybrid systems
As organizations migrate to digital platforms, they need to support and maintain their legacy systems until full migration is complete

Change IT landscape
Leverage DT projects to rid the enterprise of siloed, fragmented, and duplicated IT and data environments

Rid of technical debt
A benefit of a DT project is that it can be used to remove a legacy patchwork of timesaving upgrades and installations

The right digital platform
Spend quality time in choosing the right cloud platform in this changing, complex digital landscape

15 Testing organization maturity

It is critical to have a united vision for the business, employees, and customers to develop a great digital organization. The first step in creating that vision is evaluating your company's present level of development, which you can do with a digital maturity assessment.

Most businesses recognize that, in the digital age, a company-wide transformation is required for development and survival. Many businesses, on the other hand, are still unsure of where they are in their path. A digital maturity assessment allows tech leaders to understand where their firms are on this path and set short- and long-term goals based on that information. With technology growing at a breakneck pace, businesses must examine their digital maturity regularly. Assessment allows tech leaders to determine where their companies are in the digital transformation journey and, based on this information, set short-term and long-term goals.

A digital maturity assessment is a questionnaire that tech executives can use to figure out where their companies are on their digital transformation path. They can develop short- and long-term goals based on this knowledge for what their organizations need to do to keep up with digitalization and innovation.

A digital maturity assessment may help you understand your company's present maturity level in three dimensions (leadership and strategy, organization, and processes), as well as the main components of digital evolution. This will enable tech leaders to assess where their firm is on its digital transformation journey, set short- and long-term technology evolution priorities, create a digital transformation roadmap, and provide the groundwork for its implementation.

A BOTTLE OF WINE CONTAINS MORE
PHILOSOPHY THAN ALL THE BOOKS IN
THE WORLD.

Louis Pasteur

Testing organization maturity

Customer

Customer engagement — Customer engagement is the sending of messages to both potential & existing customers through the digital channels

Customer experience — Digital customer experience is the sum of digital interactions between a customer & a company & the resulting impression on a customer

Customer insight — Customer insight is the understanding of customers, based on their buying behaviour, their experiences & needs with you

Customer's belief — A customer's belief that a company will perform actions that will result in positive results & avoid negative outcomes

Strategy

Brand management — Digital brand management applies traditional principles to customer experiences across multiple digital mediums with focus on the customer interaction

Market intelligence — Data quality management is a organizations can leverage data to unlock new opportunities

Ecosystem management — A digital ecosystem management (DEM) solution is needed that is both smart and flexible enough to make coordinating and monetizing multi-party, multi-service platforms simple

Portfolio innovation — Innovation Portfolio Management (IPM) is a tool to convert strategic priorities & objectives into innovation activities which are project-based

Strategic management — A digital strategy specifies the direction an organization will take to create new competitive advantages &tactics to achieve these changes

Finance and investment — Having the finances for investment for digital transformation initiatives fir utilizing technology such that it re-creates into efficient operations & processes

Business assurance — Business assurance supports assuring that the things are working as planned. It has controls controls in processes & decisions

Technology

Emerging technology & applications — Emerging technologies include cloud, big data, internet of Things, nanotechnology, biotechnology, cognitive science, psychotechnology, robotics, RPA & AI

Connectivity — Connectivity makes anything possible in today's digital age, information is bringing change to everything, & connectivity is the medium through which all info is exchanged

Data management — Digital data management involves the definition and implementation of policies, practices and procedures that facilitate the effective and efficient use of digital data

Security — New technologies need new security requirements, which existing controls may or may not be able to address. And with rapid release cycles, testing capabilities must keep up with more security

Data governance — Data governance (DG) is the process of managing the availability, usability, integrity and security of the data in enterprise systems, based on internal data standards & policies for data usage.

Technology Architecture — A DT architect takes user's requirements from initial concept to an executable technical journey. Organizations need focus on the big picture plus on the details of tech. change

Operations

Agile change management — Agile changes as a project develops. That's why, in an Agile project, the planning, design, development, and testing cycles are never done

Integrated service management — Accelerate transformation with Integrated Digital Service Management (ITSM) which helps enterprises in delivering end-to-end IT services that are aligned to their goals

Real time insights and analytics — Data analytics aids automation processes for numerous applications as providing insight about when a system will fail.

Smart process management — Business process management drives transformation. A DT goal is to make existing processes more efficient & faster time to market

Culture

Organizational agility — Transformation isn't really about tech, it's about organizational agility, culture plays a vital role in the digital transformation of any business. Leadership & culture leads the adoption of technology

Digital governance and standards — Digital governance and standards are a framework for establishing accountability, roles, & decision-making authority for an organization's digital presence which means its websites, mobile sites, social channels

Employee enablement — Employee enablement is the process of taking the employees beyond the engagement stage and empowering them with the right set of tools & circumstances to deliver quality results

16 Transformation in telcos

To address the expectations of clients in this digital age, telecom companies must digitize and automate tedious processes. Traditional methods to telecom operators will not be able to keep up with this amount of change. To be relevant in the face of this paradigm shift, businesses must embrace digitalization, which combines automation, cognitive controls, and data-driven insights. Two digital streams are now converging: one from the perspective of the client, and the other from the perspective of business and operations. Telecom companies will be better positioned to benefit from digitization if they can increase the amount of synergy between these two areas.

The greatest irony of the mobile computing era is that many telecom companies that enable it still have a high amount of manual operational processes that cause consumer unhappiness. They must adopt automated procedures and systems that will allow them to respond quickly to customers to create a responsive, multifaceted, intelligent environment.

Telecom companies rely heavily on manual processes that have existed for decades. Customer unhappiness is frequently caused by operational procedures (e.g., SLA violations, extended lead times to manufacture new goods or order/provision new services). Furthermore, because these procedures are inefficient and prone to errors, they raise operational costs. Today's digital customers expect more consistent and dependable service from telecom companies, and they expect better products and customer service without demanding higher revenues, which is impossible to provide without rising operational costs.

Telecom companies may upgrade and function in a 'software defined' world with Automation Anywhere. This not only enhances client experiences, but also increases operational efficiency, lowers operating expenses, and even helps anticipate consumer wants in advance.

THE GOOD WE DO TODAY BECOMES THE
HAPPINESS OF TOMORROW.

William James

Transformation in telcos

Digital transformation

Automated work processes
Digital transformation means that key aspects of functional work performed in organizations today will be automated

More focus on knowledge based work
People will spend less time doing manual processing and focus more on higher-level, strategic and knowledge-based work

Agile organizations
Organizations will become more agile with flexible workforce supply replacing fixed organizational structures & governance

Barriers to digital transformation on Telcos

Regulatory framework
Telco regulations in individual countries can inhibit telcos' ambitions for Digital Transformation

Telco culture
Leadership, culture, skills and organizational challenges are key barriers to Telecom's digital transformation goals. The innovative inertia within telcos culture impacts their their ability to attract and retain the best digital talent for Digital Transformation initiatives

Align people, processes & technology
Aligning people, processes and skills with technology

Legacy systems
Many telcos are hindered in their DT initiatives with legacy systems

Limited collaboration
There is limited collaboration within the public & private sectors

Top 5 investment priorities

Business intelligence
Leverage the use business intelligence to transform data into actionable insights that inform an organization's strategic &tactical decisions business decisions

Customer facing applications
Ensure customer facing applications that directly interact with customers with customers add value to relationships with them and is a tool for client analytics

Customer experience management
Use CX Management to design and react to customer interactions to meet or exceed their expectations , leading to greater customer loyalty, satisfaction and advocacy

Operations support systems
Enhance operations support systems to enables improved monitoring, control, analysis, & management of network services

Customer relationship management
Leverage customer relationship management (CRM) to manage all the company's relationships and interactions (contact & sales management)

The desired future state for Telcos

Network operations agility
Increased agility with automation & ability to rapidly respond to customer requirements and new business models

Improved customer engagement
Meet customer expectations for ease of ordering, delivery and problem resolution. Make customised, relevant new offerings based on data analytics

Enable internal innovation
The need for rapid innovation means that telcos must fill key capability gaps using new innovation models & new talent strategies for a digital staff

Virtualization
Virtualization using software-defined networking will enable the use of development of low cost, self-aware, self-optimizing, self-healing cloud infrastructure networks that will be managed in a autonomous way

Beyond connectivity
Increasing digitization will provide TELCOS with key opportunities to for new revenue streams through new digital services & business models

New services
Turn operators into service aggregators like Apple app store for iPhones for third parties (e.g. media, financial services, utilities)

Fast fail mentality
Adopting DevOps and fast-fail mentality to unleash creative potential within a telco's own staff and provide an attractive environment for recruitment

Security management
Instead of an ad-hoc approach, management of security must become a central transformation consideration

Expand business partners
Evolve from a small set of suppliers to multiple set of service providers for new innovative services

Business models
Create a culture & technical environment to support multiple business models in multiple vertical markets

Open API environment
Telcos will evolve from a closed IT centric architecture for its own customer services to an open platform architecture accessed via APIs

17 CX transformation

The process of reforming a firm by putting the wants and experiences of its customers at the centre of everything it does is known as Customer (CX) transformation. Organizations that have invested in the practices, tools, and culture necessary to reliably deliver high-quality CX at scale are successful. Although it appears to be simple, many people fail to even begin.

The transformation of a company's customer experience is known as CX transformation. When a firm implements processes and technologies to satisfy the demands of its consumers, it benefits from CX transformation. CX transformation is essential for creating a customer-centric organization that also caters to the demands of employees and shareholders, yet many businesses are struggling with it today. Unfortunately, CX transformation has a high failure rate, making it a dangerous effort.

Customer journey mapping, analysing pain spots and business possibilities for the company, and balancing customer expectations versus organizational capabilities and expenses are all best to practice approaches to achieving CX transformation.

Customer experience (CX) transformation is a strategic move that strives to improve the CX on a broad scale and over time. Organizational values, structures, operations, culture, and technology will all undergo changes to ensure that they are fully aligned with customer needs and focused on delivering high-quality experiences at scale. This transformation does not occur overnight. It necessitates a solid business strategy and an even stronger execution plan that educates all employees in the formation of good habits, allows them to collaborate smoothly toward company goals, and equips them with the necessary tools and processes.

THE HAPPINESS OF YOUR LIFE DEPENDS UPON THE QUALITY OF YOUR THOUGHTS.

Marcus Aurelius

CX transformation

CX strategy

Customer experience (CX) — Customer experience (CX) refers to the sum of every interaction a customer has with a business, both pre- and post-sale

Customer experience strategy — The CX strategy defines the actionable plans in place to deliver a positive, meaningful experience across those interactions

Customer experience strategy plan — A CX strategy plan guides activities & resources required to deliver customer experiences aligned to business goals

CX service

- Be accountable
- Be personal
- Be innovative
- Be empathetic
- Be trustworthy

Customer service improvements

A clear CX vision — Create a clear customer experience vision

Know your customers — Understand your customers (who they are, desires))

Build an emotional customer connection — Develop an emotional customer connection

Real time customer feedback — Capture real time customer feedback

Make customer experience a core skill — Make quality CX part of staff goals

Regular feedback to develop employees — Use regular feedback to hone staff CX skills

CX transformation

Loyal customers — Engaged loyal customers

Competitive advantage — Via multiple integrated touchpoints

Streamlined services — Streamline customer service

Improved performance — Improved business performance

Interactions — At every touchpoint, personalisation

Elements of CX transformation

CX vision — Create clear desired CX vision

CX governance team — To align on CX priorities and actions

CX roadmap — Develop roadmap of CX initiatives

CX metrics — CX metrics to measure progress

Change management — Develop CX change plan

Customer experience assessment steps

Leadership commitment to customer experience — Determine how much committed to improving CX

Existing CX maturity — Assess existing CX maturity & develop CX roadmap

Existing CX projects — Identify existing CX projects, capabilities & tech

Get the basic CX right and innovate — Make basic CX good and identify new ideas

CX projects are measures — Review existing CX projects & metrics

The head of customer experience — If role doesn't exist, create one for focus

CX leadership governance group — Invite stakeholders for a CX leadership governance

Customer experience metrics — Create a customer experience leader dashboard

Review existing talent & skills for CX — Review firm for CX and tech skills

Customer experience best practices

- Company customer focus DNA
- Company alignment for CX focus
- Assess CX model (people, process, systems and data)
- Personalize CX experiences
- Customer data based decisions
- Design from customer viewpoint
- Eliminate silos across business
- Enable seamless omnichannel CX
- Integrate & digitize processes
- Link CX to business outcomes
- Keep the human touch

Customer experience management

Customer experience management — CX managers organise, plan, & monitor a firm's customer service to improve customer interactions

Customer experience platform — It is a digital technology CX software platform solution that allows businesses to measure, manage & improve customer experience

Customer experience management — CX Management is the design and reaction to customer interactions in order to meet or exceed customer expectations

CX metrics

Net promoter score (NPS) — Track customer loyalty over time

Customer satisfaction (CSAT) — Measures if a client is satisfied with one-time interaction

Customer effort score (CES) — "How easy was it to solve your issue?"

18 Driving creativity & innovation

Both creativity and innovation are vital for corporate success and are linked but distinct ideas. Many people mistakenly believe that creativity and innovation are the same things, yet they are not. Creativity is the process of coming up with a novel idea or developing a previously unsolved problem. It might be interpreted as the emergence of new thinking or idea, or as a previously unnoticed insight. Innovation, on the other hand, is the process of bringing about change through new methods of performing tasks and utilizing resources. Processes, technology, and products may all be affected.

Problem-solving skills are enhanced by creativity. It makes no difference whether we're talking about creating a new strategy or coming up with fresh ways to keep ahead of the competition. Creative issue solution provides the competitive advantage that every company strives for. Many companies produce well-designed items, but coming up with a novel idea necessitates creative thought. Many people fail because they do not properly reach their objectives.

Organizational structure, culture, and mentality, evaluating innovation, reward and recognition systems, lack of top management engagement, inability to involve all staff, insufficient money, and lack of skills required to report invention are all examples of failure.

The requirements for driving innovation initiatives differ significantly from those that apply to other sorts of projects. Driving innovation entails initiating something new and unfamiliar that will add value. The first electric vehicles to hit the market were likewise ground-breaking, and new batteries with longer ranges continue to emerge. Technology is propelled by creativity and invention. Our future will be shaped by the ingenuity and invention of today's developers, programmers, artists, and designers.

IN THE SMALL MATTERS TRUST THE MIND,
IN THE LARGE ONES THE HEART.

Sigmund Freud

Driving Creativity & Innovation

Innovation

Service innovation
Service Innovation is due to the digitalisation efforts in many areas

Process innovation
Process Innovation has been a BPM activity in organizations for many years

Business model
Business model innovation often uses Osterwalder's Business Model Canvas

Problem driven
Innovation driven is by a problem (bottlenecks, costs, services times)

Constraint innovation
Driven by a constraint of boundaries within the context of an organization

Opportunity driven innovation
Innovation driven by an opportunity are borne out of the realisation of a possibility.

Team innovation
An innovative team examines existing products to leverage their diverse knowledge & skillsets, ideates and executes improvements

Personal innovation
Personal innovation has the aim of making a world a better one. Personal innovation can be on a professional or personal level

Types of innovation

Incremental innovation
It uses existing technology and increases value to the customer (features, design changes)

Disruptive innovation
This involves applying new technology (often inferior) or processes to the current market

Architectural innovation
This simply take the lessons, skills and tech. and applying them within a different market.

Radical innovation
This gives birth to new industries & involves creating revolutionary technology

innovation challenges

Lack of staff empowerment
Staff not empowered to innovate

Lack of employee motivation
Staff aren't motivated to innovate

Lack of an innovation strategy
A strategy for innovation & execution

Innovation to one group
Innovation is centralized to one group

Lack of collaboration
Collaboration is the key to innovation (Int. & Ext.)

Diversity within organisation
Diverse teams can provide a wealth of ideas

Complacent with the current state
Current products / service are already successful

Lack of customer empathy
Customer empathy is key to stay abreast of trends

Innovation benefits

- Competitive advantage
- Increased value
- Increased value add (usp)
- Employee retention
- Reduced costs
- Better quality products
- improved productivity
- Industry leadership
- New products & services
- Brand recognition

Workplace innovation

Ways to connect people to firm
When people are connected to a company, more incentive for them to be innovative

Employee decision making
Empower your employees to have the responsibility make decisions and take action

Remove red tape
Too many organizations have such bureaucratic processes that makes it difficult to promote ideas

Use Walt Disney brainstorming
Use the 3 roles of Disney to play the dreamer, the realist, & the spoiler in brainstorming

Use a 'day in a life' method
As a combination of research & storytelling, the "Day in the Life" method is very valuable for insights

Create workplace for creativity
Create a workplace environment that makes it easy for employees to have and share ideas

Calm the organisation naysayers
Make sure to create an environment to make it safe to brainstorm and not shoot down new ideas

A leadership role model
If leaders never demonstrates thinking creatively, how can they expect their staff to be innovative

Be an innovator

Do new or different things
Being innovative means doing things differently or doing things that have never been done before

Dynamic value based leadership
Innovative leaders hire staff who love their work and gives them opportunities to grow

Innovators & collaboration
They see collaboration as opportunity to value, build and sustain active, vibrant people networks

Innovators embrace diversity
Innovators embraces diversity & understand it takes many different points of view for new ideas

Personal innovation

Surround with inspiration
Whenever you see something that inspires, put it on display

Pick small ideas opportunities
Lots of small ideas can add up to make a big difference in benefits

Bring your ideas to life
Stop thinking, put your thoughts into words, pictures, & prototypes

Get out of the office
Make a habit of going outside for a walk in a park and make a point to be aware

19 Agile leadership

Visionary, action-oriented, and democratic are three words that define an agile leader. Strategic focus is combined with practical implementation and team empowerment is the essence of a successful agile leader. They strive to establish a safe environment in which their employees may perform at their best, as well as give coaching to help them reach their full potential. Any organization's success depends on its ability to lead with agility. Agile leaders set the tone for their organizations, are action-oriented, set clear goals for their teams, dismantle departmental silos, and encourage employees to work flexibly. Agile leaders have a growth mentality and strive to be lifelong learners who are continually growing as leaders. The capacity to lead with agility is critical to any organization's success.

Agile leaders set the tone for their organizations by being action-oriented, setting clear goals for their teams, breaking down departmental walls, and encouraging workers to work flexibly. Agile leaders have a growth mindset and seek to be lifelong learners and leaders that are always learning.

Agile leadership aims to remove impediments to success for staff to be more effective and productive. Agile leadership generates better business outcomes with less wasted time and resources because agile teams operate better together. By breaking down departmental silos that frequently stifle innovation, creativity, and the fulfilment of potential, agile working enables businesses to reach the new frontiers they need to explore and find in these changing and tough business times. Agile leaders are continually seeking ways to push their teams, striving to improve based on experience and the belief that change is both feasible and important. They steer their organizations in the right direction while remaining action-oriented, creating clear goals for their employees and dismantling departmental silos.

PATIENCE IS THE STRENGTH OF THE
WEAK, IMPATIENCE IS THE WEAKNESS OF
THE STRONG.

Immanuel Kant

Agile leadership

Leadership styles

Autocratic leadership
A task-oriented "command and control" style. They set clear expectations & directions to staff, tell them what to do

Delegative leadership
A people-oriented leadership style is delegative. The leader doesn't provide much direction; decisions are made by staff.

Democratic leadership
A mix of the task-oriented and people-oriented leadership styles. The leader provides guidance & direction, asks for feedback

Agile leadership
Agile leadership is about self-organisation where agile teams collaborate, learn from each other, get quick feedback from users.

Companies going agile

Faster delivery
A primary reason firms want to speed up software delivery

Able for changing priorities
Have greater ability to manage changing priorities by being able to adapt quickly

Productivity
By ensuring building right products efficiently as possible

IT/ business alignment
With greater stakeholder involvement at all stages results in better alignment

Software quality
A better approach in agile as quality is fixed, & scope & sequence are variable

Agile leaders

Focus n action
They are more around doing

Remove roadblocks
Focus removing barriers

Constant learning
They are constantly learning

Focus on people
They focus on people

Comms skills
A passion for comms & listening skills

Strong focus on priorities
An agile leader knows what to focus on

Drive and inspire
Ability to drive & inspire staff

time for reflection
They use reflection to think and learn

Openness & honesty
Clear ethics of ethics and integrity

Plan as they go
Plan & strategize as they go not before

Make decisions quickly
With limited information, make decisions fast

Create learning environment
Agile leaders aim to increase learning & adjust thinking on that learning

Visible & transparent
Make things visible & transparent

Flexibility
Use a high degree of flexibility in how they structure, organize, & execute the work

Feedback
Know how to give, receive and encourage useful feedback from staff

Create conditions
To promote collaboration & ownership

Introducing new practices
Providing coaching & mentoring staff to become better adapting their plans to unplanned changes in software delivery

Sets out new roles
An agile leader sets out new roles that describes specific skills sets that many staff need to ensure a more efficient flow of work

Agile styles

An Agile Leader promotes a shared vision for an agile organisation to be successful & provide a way forward of continual improvement

Coaching
Agile leaders focus on coaching and helping others in their development

Focus on process & quality
Quality, metrics to improve things & introducing new practices

Organizational shared vision
Facilitates orientation around a shared vision (town halls, group lunches, 'break-outs', outside speakers

Organizational barriers
They understand the challenges & barriers teams run into, and help their teams overcome these barriers

Agile mindset

Respect
Respect starts with team members & goes to staff at all levels of organization

Collaboration
Collaboration is key to solve complex issues & at organisation level will reduce handoffs to deliver

Continuous improvement
No process or leadership style or way of working is written in stone. Always room for improvement

Learning to fail
Allowing staff to try new ideas & possibly fail, gives staff an opportunity to learn and improve

Pride in ownership
Pride in what is delivered increases the desire to deliver quality work

Focus on delivering value
An agile team focuses on delivering the greatest value to customer

Ability to adapt to change
If unplanned changes are need, the organization adapts with it

20 Cloud migration considerations

The process of migrating data and applications to a cloud computing environment such as Amazon Web Services is known as cloud migration (AWS). The movement of data from an on-premises or co-located data centre to the public cloud is a popular model. The process of transferring software applications from one domain to another is known as application migration. Access to on-demand computing resources, increased efficiency, cost savings, and improved performance are all advantages of cloud migration.

When considering a cloud migration, keep in mind the business benefits of cloud computing and how it can help your company become more flexible. While in terms of technology, the focus is on minimizing operational and capital costs to save money. Every company is different, with its own set of wants and expectations. When planning your migration to the public cloud, whether you're relocating a few virtual machines (VMs) or re-architecting your physical data centre, there are a few things to keep in mind.

When migrating to the cloud, it's crucial to think about how you'll use it and what your business requirements are. Understanding the differences between on-premise and cloud computing necessitates a balanced strategy that considers security, cost, and accessibility, among other factors. When transferring data or apps to the cloud, there are several factors to consider and plan for before moving forward.

Moving your company to the cloud is a major undertaking. It might be difficult to know how to make the best selections for your company when there are so many products, technology, and deployment options available. Moving data and applications from a local data centre to the public cloud can result in increased innovation, analytics, storage flexibility, and cost savings. However, it is not an easy task. To move smoothly, you'll need to make important infrastructure decisions and even handle cultural shifts inside your company.

CHANGE IS NEVER PAINFUL, ONLY THE
RESISTANCE TO CHANGE IS PAINFUL.

Gautama Buddha

Cloud migration considerations

Cloud migration considerations

Migration strategy
Moving applications to the cloud requires a good strategy for leadership, technology & resources.

Data and application inventory
Take an inventory of data & applications, identify dependencies & consider which is the best migration option for your needs & organisation

The cost of cloud migration
If an an firm has large investment in hardware & software licensing, it is worth considering to migrate to cloud or not

The best cloud option
Decide whether a public, private, hybrid or even a multi-cloud scenario with IaaS options meets the needs of your firm

Application performance requirements
Decide performance needs (bandwidth, dependencies) for applications in the cloud

Redundant features and stale data
Cloud migration offers an opportunity to do some data cleaning by removing stale data

Staff realignment for cloud migration
Migrating applications to the cloud requires different leadership and strong technical skills

Cloud migration challenges

Business continuity
A cloud migration challenge can impact business continuity arises from failing to plan for issues such as drive failures

Data and application portability
The flexibility of data & applications to be portably installed, deployed, accessed and managed without major rework

Data integrity
Data integrity in cloud storage is most critical concern of cloud clients. Assurance of data integrity means data remain as it is on server for long time.

Interoperability
Interoperability is the ability of an firm to use the same management tools, server images and other software with a variety of cloud computing providers

Refactoring applications can be costly
Moving an application to cloud without any modifications (Lift-and-shift migration) but may not work for performance issues, refactoring it can be too costly sometimes

Cost containment
Many firms that lift and shift their applications to Cloud IaaS without optimisation will over provision by up to 50% during the first 18 months, will overspend & have cost overruns by a large margin

Lack of visibility & control
The loss of service visibility & control in the cloud can mean a loss of control over many aspects of IT management & data security can lead to failing to identify risks

Data breaches and downtime
Cloud services are more secure than legacy architecture, but still a potential risk in data breaches a& downtime, a business has little control over how long critical business systems may be offline or how well the breach is managed

Vendor lock-in
For companies who rely heavily on a cloud platform, there is a danger of vendor lock in forced to continue with a specific third-party vendor

Compliance complexity
In some sectors , where legislative laws with regard to storage of private data are heavy, achieving full compliance whilst cloud offerings can be more complex.

A lack of transparency from cloud providers
When a business uses a cloud service, they do not get a full service description, on how the platform works & the security processes. This lack of transparency makes it hard for a business to evaluate whether its data is stored securely

Insecure interfaces
Cloud vendors provide users a range of (APIs), to manage the cloud service but not every API is secure so a potential data security threat

Insufficient due diligence
Some businesses lack the resources to fully evaluate the implications of cloud adoption, then deploying is a real risk

Shared technology risks
Using a cloud can expose a business to security risks caused by other users of the same cloud infrastructure causes a security vulnerability that will affect every user

Other security risks
A man in the middle attack is where a 3rd party becomes a relay of data between a source & a destination

Cloud migration process

Choosing a cloud provider
Each loud provider has their strengths & weaknesses. Cost, level of service and capacity demands are factors

Preparing to migrate to the cloud
Proper planning the most important stage of the process. Move the easiest, least critical apps first. Will your Enterprise Architecture need to change for migration? Has performance and downtime for users been considered with migration? Are required staff skills in place for cloud migration & support? Are new operating procedures in place for troubleshooting, updates, metrics? Governance, security procedures re-evaluated?

Migrating to the cloud
How is data going to be moved? What security processes in place for moving data? Have you the right tool to move data and databases? Any sort of IT migration is dangerous !

Did the migration work?
Is there an an automated testing strategy to test the migration worked? Did all of the data make it? Is it all reachable to business users? Is everything communicating properly? Do not be tempted to do it on the cheap

NOTHING GREAT WAS
EVER ACHIEVED
WITHOUT ENTHUSIASM.

Ralph Waldo Emerson

21 Operational excellence

A successful business is built on operational excellence. Whether you want to cut expenses, improve quality, or increase customer acquisition and retention, operational excellence can help you get there.

Operational excellence is defined as consistently and reliably executing the business plan than the competition. It entails ensuring that firm operations are well-designed, regulated, and measured; that employees are focused on creating value; and that everyone is empowered to enhance performance continuously. It is a mindset that adopts specific concepts and methods to foster an organizational culture of excellence. Every person must be able to perceive, provide, and improve the flow of value to a client to achieve operational excellence.

As a result, concentrating on process efficiency, customer value creation, and business growth is three elements of operational excellence.

A successful business's ability to execute its strategy more consistently and reliably than the competition is a crucial differentiator. This necessitates a well-structured, well-resourced strategy that instils operational excellence into the company's culture.

Delivering superior value via continuous improvement of all processes, people, goods, and services is what operational excellence is all about. It's all about being innovative, trying to be the greatest, pushing for greatness, and constantly improving. Operational excellence involves eliminating processes and inefficiencies that restrict or obstruct a company's ability to achieve its goals and objectives. As a result, a company with good operational performance can offer products and services at a lower price than its competitors. Depending on the industry and the age of the program, the success of an operational excellence program can be measured in a variety of ways.

Customers' satisfaction, process improvements, and cost reductions were the top three success indicators cited by leadership in several firms.

YOU MUST LOOK INTO PEOPLE,
AS WELL AS AT THEM.

Lord Chesterfield

Key questions for operational excellence

Exec support
How committed is senior management to outstanding process?

Exec comms
How do leaders communicate and demonstrate their commitment to operational excellence?

Governance
Is there a communication and governance structure in place to support continuous improvement initiatives?

Staff engagement
What do leaders do to facilitate better engagement with employees for the benefit of operational excellence? Are there metrics in place to measure the effectiveness of engagement?

CI DNA in firm
Is continuous improvement part of the DNA of the organisation? Is everyone expected to spend a small percentage of time on improving the business? What do staff & customers think?

Processes
How often does senior management meet to discuss with employees "How to do things better to improve processes?"

Changes
How are changes to processes reviewed, implemented and communicated throughout our organization?

Optimization
Is there investment in optimizing operations in terms of tools, capabilities and incentives for teams?

Process owners
Are process owners identified and empowered to continually strive for operational excellence?

Centralized tool
Is there a centralised process management tool that is easily accessible by everyone in the organization, to engage employees in their process improvement efforts?

Key factors for operational excellence

Competitive edge — The execution of the business strategy better than the competition.

Culture of value — Creating a culture of goal setting, value add, flexibility and continuous improvement.

Process focus — A big focus on reinventing processes with the goal of lowering costs, reducing cycle times, and increasing quality using new tech & data.

PMO operations — The PMO needs a clear PM Methodology to establish consistency in project delivery supported by tools to promote knowledge transfer.

Changing priorities — Ability to manage changing priorities through the ability to adapt quickly.

More productivity — Building the right products as efficiently as possible.

Improved costs — Cost & benefits analysis on business improvement opportunities.

Goals & KPIs — Goals & KPIs measured &d reported with greater frequency and accuracy.

Clear roles — Clearly defined roles and responsibilities (RACI).

Real time activities — Real-time involvement in operational activities & issues requiring tactical decision making.

Desired state for operational excellences

Customer needs
The organisation continually assesses and updates capabilities to meet current and emerging customer needs.

Exec support
Leadership demonstrates its commitment to operational excellence and enhanced customer experience.

Best practices
There is a continual search for operational excellence best practices that produce superior results.

Automation
Process tools provide automation to improve the efficiency of basic core processes which are optimised for value add to effectively facilitate the enhanced customer experience.

Focus on process
The primary focus is on process excellence, process ownership and performance for improving results.

Holistic viewpoint
Processes are viewed in a holistic end to end view to provide business insights.

Reduced costs
Costs are being continually reduced through automation and process improvement.

Enterprise tool
An enterprise tool is implemented for monitoring the quality of employee performance in terms of KPIs.

Staff satisfaction
Improved employee satisfaction through empowerment and process owners to take necessary action to solve process issues. Training and coaching are implemented to optimise the performance and productivity of employees.

Feedback process
There is an effective feedback and reward process for staff to submit ideas and suggestions for improvement.

MY BEST FRIEND IS A
PERSON WHO WILL GIVE ME
A BOOK I HAVE NOT READ.

Abraham Lincoln

Operational excellence

Definitions

- **Corporate strategy** — "What business should we be in?"
- **Business strategy** — "How to compete in this business?"
- **Operational excellence** — The execution of business strategy better than competition

Operational excellence

- **Operational excellence is not…** It is neither a specific management philosophy or methodology
- **Drivers to enable excellence** — It integrates continuous improvement organizational structure & leadership
- **Evidenced by results for operational excellence** — An OE company has lower operational risk, lower operating costs, & increased revenues vs. competitors & creating value for clients

Strategy (Hoshin Kanri process)

- **Vision & TOBE** — Assess mission, vision & "TO BE" processes
- **Stretch goals** — The firm to stretch in new ways (3-5 yrs.)
- **Annual goals** — Set annual goals to reach 3-5 year target goals
- **Cascade goals** — Assign dept, & staff goals that align to mission
- **Execute goals** — Actions & use of tools to meet annual goals
- **Monthly reviews** — Check on each person's progress to goals regularly
- **Annual review** — Assess year end of the firm's progress on goals

Performance management

- **4th generation balanced scorecards** — These scorecards accepts leadership is agile & not just measured by targets. Staff needs empowerment & customers treated as equals
- **Gemba kaizen** (a Japanese form of continuous improvement. Gemba refers to location where value is created, while Kaizen relates to improvements

Process excellence

Operational Excellence is having simple, fast, repeatable business processes and ensuring the company is continuously improving its operations

Value stream mapping (Used to identify and remove or reduce "waste" in value streams)

Faster than needed	Conveyance	Corrected mistakes
Waiting time	Unnecessary motion	Unneeded work
		Excess stock

SIPOC (a business process from start to end)

- Supplier
- Input
- Process
- Output
- Customer

Organizations excellence (McKinsey 7S)

Operational Excellence is establishing the most effective organization structure aligned with the culture & leadership, with clear roles & responsibilities

- **Shared values** — The standards that guide employee's behaviour company actions
- **Style** — The firms leaders style & symbolic values
- **Staff** — Type, how many staff & how recruited, trained & rewarded
- **Skills** — The abilities that employees perform very well
- **Systems** — The processes which do the business daily activities
- **Structure** — How business is organized & who is accountable
- **Strategy** — A plan to achieve sustained competitive advantage

Leadership, people and culture

Operational Excellence is having the right people and leadership & competences, establishing the right culture & enabling behaviours for the strategy

- **People** — A company is its culture & people who share and embraces its core values
- **Leadership** — It's the engine that drives culture every day by leaders from top to bottom
- **Practices** — These are "Walk The Talk", if people are your greatest asset," – invest in them
- **Values** — Values are guidelines on the behaviours and mindsets needed
- **Vision** — A vision statement helps orient customers, suppliers & stakeholders
- **Culture** — A culture that promotes the desired behaviours

Shingo prize operational excellence

1. Respect every individual
2. Lead with humility
3. Seek perfection
4. Assure quality at the source
5. Flow and pull value
6. Use scientific thinking
7. Focus on process
8. Think systems
9. Create constancy of purpose
10. Create value for the customer

22 Business agility

Companies seek to develop their company and provide a fantastic customer experience by fast organizing to stay relevant to customers. Business agility refers to a company's ability to respond quickly to market changes and seize new possibilities. Companies that react fast to changing customer trends can adapt their operations to become more customer-centric, resulting in a better customer experience. Business agility entails a company's capacity to organize itself in such a way that it remains relevant and fulfils changing needs.

Agility in an organization's culture, leadership, strategy, and governance that offers value to all stakeholders who operate in uncertain, complicated, and ambiguous situations is defined as business agility. Business agility not only assists you in adapting to market changes but also assists you in adapting to internal changes. Furthermore, company agility evolves and changes in tandem with the market, allowing it to react to developments and trends. Having a structure in place to prepare your company for change makes you even more powerful.

When market conditions change, business agility relates to adaptability, which can help organizations stay competitive and successful. Business agility can be achieved by implementing successful strategies and setting targets that are guided by the company mission. Using big data and analytics to help you make better decisions is one of the most important parts of agility. Manufacturing companies dealing with supply chain interruptions are a good example of this.

Advanced processes, tools, and training are used by highly agile organizations to enable successful replies to the advent of new competitors, rapid technological breakthroughs, and sudden adjustments in general market conditions. They thrive in companies that aren't hierarchical and don't have a single point of management.

HE THAT FALLS IN LOVE
WITH HIMSELF WILL
HAVE NO RIVALS.

Benjamin Franklin

Business agility

An agile business

An agile business is customer centric
An agile business embraces the agile philosophy & values at its core, from its people & culture, to its structure

Roles
Agile businesses have roles instead of job descriptions

Dynamic decisions
Agile businesses have fluid roles to make active decisions

Use agile methods
Agile business address the issues of complexity, & uncertainty by planning & executing in parallel

Temporary competitive advantage
An Agile business chases a series of temporary competitive advantages instead of following a sustained competitive advantage

Embraces agile concepts
Agile businesses have self-organizing teams which bring together all parts of the business

People driven to learn new expertise
Agile staff focus to be expert in one area but are driven to develop expertise next "new" areas

Agile in DNA
Business vision, & values has agile in DNA

Able to adapt quickly
Agile businesses have ability to adapt quickly when their environment changes

Flexible organization & business processes
Agile businesses have a flexible organization structure and business processes to adapt to customer or supplier base changes

Agile businesses have shared structures
Agile businesses gain structure by a having a shared vision, resource management systems, reward systems, and shared operating platforms

Fluid movement of resources
Agile businesses achieve fluid movement of resources via a process of having enterprise values, personal accountability, & motivational and staff reward systems

Holacracy (A method of decentralised management & governance)
Agile businesses tend to use holacracy which authority and decision-making is distributed throughout the company as a holacracy of self-organizing teams rather than being vested in a management hierarchy

Makes change routine
The agile enterprise strives to make change a routine part of organizational life

Agile businesses use agile software development
The use agile software development where requirements & solutions evolve through the collaborative effort of cross-functional teams & stakeholders

Enterprise Architecture (EA)
Agile business EA supports business agility through a wealth of techniques, and the separation of dynamic and stable components

Agile business benefits

Agile reduces trauma
An agile business reduces trauma that paralyzes many businesses trying to adapt

Products in a state of change
Products are constantly changing, as they run into competitors' products, regulators, suppliers, & customer responses

Self organized teams
Self-organizing teams, found within agile enterprises, are the spontaneous, not planned or directed, feedback-driven exchanges that occur between them

Coevolution
Coevolution is a key process where the influence of closely associated enterprise teams on each other from experience and adaption

Catalyst leadership
Uses style to inspire others with out losing cohesion of enterprise

Focus on real value
Agile methodologies focus on driving real business value, not just features

Ability to adapt to changes quickly
An agile business can react successfully to the emergence of new competitors, new technology & shifts in overall market conditions

Governance based on value
Governance within an agile business is based upon long-term business value and adaptation

Shortening of time to market
The need to shorten delivery times of new services & shortening of competitor's time to market for new services

Customised services
Customers are demanding more tailored and customised services and products

Changing requirements
Changing requirements taking too long to implement into the organization & processes

Need for lower prices
A growing need for lower priced products & services with price wars & lower margins global competition

Move to digitalization
Demand for more online and self service facilities for customer buying & requests

Complexity of processes
Owing to interdependencies with other units & other services

Financial transparency
A demand for financial transparency and accountability

Decreasing loyalty
Decreasing loyalty of customers

Drivers

- Fast changes of technology
- More partnerships
- Need lean processes
- Quicker response times
- Maximum use of resources

23 Your organization agility

Organizational agility is defined as the ability to sense and adapt quickly and effectively to volatile market conditions, aligning the company by integrating people, processes, and technology in a way that ensures high levels of performance are maintained over time. It necessitates agility at all levels of the organization, from individual employees (and supporting technology) to teams, critical departments, and finally the entire company.

Companies that are agile focus on what matters to their customers. They do what adds the most value to their companies, and they give their employees the freedom and autonomy they need to succeed. A phrase used to describe firms that are quick to respond to changes in the marketplace or environment is "agile." The agile company is focused on the needs of its customers, which necessitate customized rather than standardized solutions.

Agility at work requires the ability to break down barriers in the workplace to meet changing company needs, breakthroughs, or technology. Using an agile approach to projects and programs yields better results in less time, at lower cost and risk. That's because agile allows you to stay focused on what matters and adjust to new knowledge as it becomes available, rather than what you projected at the outset. Any agile change at the corporate level must be both broad and iterative.

In today's commercial world, change is happening at a breakneck speed. Business executives must guide their companies through complex, large-scale change efforts that are always changing. Restructuring, new technology and system development, fundamental transformations in work processes and practices, and changes in leadership or corporate strategy are examples of these projects.

HOPE IS A WAKING
DREAM.

Aristotle

Your organization agility

Business need questions	**Pressures for change** — How often does your industry experience pressures to change?	**Pace of change** — What is the rate the pace of change in your industry?	**Requests for change** — How often do your customers /or suppliers demand change?	**Customer feedback** — Are you listening to customer feedback to ensure you are satisfying their needs?	**Speed to business agility** — How quickly does the business need to become Agile?
The drivers for change	**Increased innovation** — Quickening pace of innovation of products and services from new & emerging technologies	**Self service demand** — Demand for more online and self-service facilities for customer buying & request	**Lower prices** — A need for lower priced products with price wars & lower margins from changing markets	**Shorter delivery times** — Shorten delivery times of new services & shortening of competitor's time to market for new and innovative services	**Demand for tailored services** — Customers are demanding more tailored and customised services and products
Business simplicity	**Governance processes** — Your governance processes enable teams to promptly respond to customer needs?	**Focus on value** — Your teams built generating value to the customer?	**Team empowerment** — Teams & individuals are empowered to respond to change requested by a customer promptly?	**Clear roles & responsibilities** — Your team members are clear on their roles & how they contribute to desired customer outcomes & business performance?	**Leadership commitment** — Your leadership is committed to introducing structural simplicity to deliver value to the customer?
Appetite for change	**Commitment to change** — How high is the leadership commitment to change?	**Company readiness** — How ready is the organization for change?	**Past change success** — How successful has change been in the past endeavours?	**Relationship development** — Is the organization developing relationships with suppliers to enable faster innovation?	**Risk impact of no change** — How high is the risk of not changing your business?
Delivering value	**Product exploration** — What % of your project portfolio is devoted to Product exploration?	**Tested assumptions** — Are assumptions, (i.e. through the release of an MVP) ?	**Customer value** — How confident are you that teams are identifying customer value?	**Product roadmaps** — Are product roadmaps evolving to support customer needs?	**Customer value blockers** — Are there blockers preventing customer value being delivered at pace?
Measures	**Goals distribution** — Are the organization's business goals and success metrics cascaded to all depts?	**Alignment to goals** — Do team members know that their work is connected to the business objectives?	**Team engagement** — Are employees engaged knowing their work impacts business objectives and success?	**MVP customer satisfaction** — Once the MVP is released, how would customer satisfaction be rated to prove that it solves a desired problem	**Value stream mapping** — Are all value streams clearly mapped out and identified?
Innovation	**Innovation** — Are staff given the opportunity to pursue new ideas & strategies?	**New products** — How many new product are evidence of teams taking risks?	**Lessons learned** — How many releases are evidence of learning from mistakes?	**Employee confidence** — How do employees feel about sharing their experiences & opinions for innovation?	**Focus on problem solving** — 'Does the organization support solving problems , to foster a 'safe to fail' culture?
Culture	**Change communications** — Does leadership communicate why change is needed in engaging ways?		**Investment in lean and agile** — Does leadership invest in in Lean and Agile principles?	**Leadership agile support** — Does leadership actively advocate Lean '7 Agile practices?	

24 Develop vision and strategy

A strategic vision is an organization's ability to establish a goal or purpose, select long-term objectives, conduct a thorough analysis of its performance in comparison to its industry competitors and the overall economy, and set parameters for value and growth. What you wish to achieve is your vision. The mission is a broad statement about how you intend to realize your vision. Strategies are a set of tactics for achieving the vision by utilizing the mission. Goals are assertions of what must be completed to put the plan into action.

We all have procedures, no matter what the goal is, whether it's to increase performance, project management, process management, or anything else. What criteria will you use to determine your success? This question has two parts: how to measure and how will you know if it works. Efforts to improve one may suffocate the other if business strategies and operating processes are not aligned.

For process management to be successful, it must be measured. First and foremost, you must specify what you wish to achieve. How will you know if everything is going according to plan? You must establish specific objectives that allow you to assess how the project is progressing

The Process Classification Framework® (PCF) is a taxonomy that groups corporate processes into a 1,001-step hierarchy. The PCF establishes a standard language for process management activities and can assist firms in identifying potential for cost savings and improved operations. The PCF can also be used as a benchmarking tool, allowing users to compare their firms to other high-performing businesses (using APQC's Open Standards Benchmarking® database).

BE KIND, FOR EVERYONE
YOU MEET IS FIGHTING A
HARDER BATTLE.

Plato

Develop vision and strategy

Develop business concept & long term vision

Assess external environment
- Identify competitors
- Analyse and evaluate competition
- Identify economic trends
- Identify political regulatory issues
- New technology innovations
- Social & cultural changes
- Identify ecological concerns
- Evaluate IP acquisition options

Survey market and assess different customer needs
- Conduct qualitative/quantitative research and assessments
- Capture and assess customer needs and wants

Assess the internal environment
- Analyse firm characteristics
- Analyse internal operations
- Create baselines for ASIS processes
- Analyse systems and technology
- Analyse financial health
- Identify core competencies

Reorganization structuring opportunities
- Identify restructuring opportunities
- Perform due-diligence
- Analyse deal options
- Evaluate acquisition options
- Evaluate merger & de-merger options

Establish strategic vision
- Define the strategic vision
- Align and communicate strategic vision to stakeholders

Develop business strategy

Mission statement
- Define current business
- Formulate mission
- Communicate mission

Define and evaluate options for strategic objectives
- Define strategic options
- Analyse each option impact
- Develop strategy
- Identify changes for business
- Identify tech. impacts
- Services strategy
- Partner strategy
- Merger / acquisition / Innovation strategy
- Global support strategy
- Shared services strategy
- Improvement strategy

Strategy & organization design
- Select long-term business strategy
- Coordinate and align functional & process strategies
- Create organizational design
- Evaluate breadth and depth of organizational structure
- Perform job-specific roles mapping & value- added analyses
- Develop role activity diagrams to assess hand- off activity
- Perform organization redesign workshops
- Develop role analysis and activity diagrams for key processes
- Migrate to new organization

Business goals & customer service strategy
- Organizational goals
- Baseline metrics
- Monitor performance
- Analyse business unit strategies
- Identify business unit competencies
- Refine business unit strategies
- Assess client experience & issues
- Review customer touch points

Design customer experience & support structure
- Create customer journey maps
- Define single view of the customer
- Define a vision for the customer experience
- Align experience to brand values & strategy
- Develop content strategy & capabilities
- Identify impact on functional processes
- Develop customer experience roadmap
- Communicate strategies internally and externally

Execute & measure strategic objectives

Develop strategic initiatives
- Identify strategic priorities
- Develop strategic initiatives on customer value
- Review with stakeholders

Evaluate strategic initiatives
- Determine business value for each strategic priority
- Determine the customer value for each strategic priority

Select strategic initiatives
- Prioritise strategic initiatives
- Communicate strategic initiatives to business stakeholders

High level measures & strategy
- Identify business value drivers
- Establish baselines for business value drivers
- Monitor performance

Develop & maintain business models

Develop business models
- Assemble business model information
- Secure appropriate approvals
- Identify integration points with existing models
- Adopt the business model

Maintain and establish business model governance
- Establish business model maintenance parameters
- Accept business feedback parameters
- Prioritise and manage incoming feedback
- Update existing models

25 Strategic alignment

Strategic alignment is a procedure that guarantees that an organization's structure, resource allocation (and culture) are in line with its plan. Organizational strategic alignment, in its most basic form, is the process of aligning a company's strategy with its culture. Awareness of the larger environment, regulatory issues, and technological development is also required for successful outcomes. By optimizing the operation of processes/systems, as well as the activities of teams and departments, strategic alignment helps to increased performance. The importance of precise, measurable operational objectives that can be linked to superordinate goals is supported by goal-setting theory. This ensures that resources are utilized efficiently.

It is not enough to have a strategy to drive business performance. According to research, having a strategy has little effect on corporate performance. What makes a difference is how well activities are executed and aligned with your strategies.

This alignment guarantees that the appropriate amount of attention is given to the appropriate activities and that nothing falls through the gaps. Not only will having a clear link between strategic and operational planning help execution, but it will also provide more transparency throughout your company.

The degree of alignment between strategy, actions, and initiatives across your business determines the strength of your organization's foundation. By uniting people and systems to meet corporate goals and objectives, strategic alignment helps you create clear focus and direction. The combination of internal and external strategy, as well as organizational capabilities, to create a product or service that matches the needs of your customers is known as strategic alignment. It is the process of connecting a company's actions, capabilities, and resources to its business strategies. Your product or service may be the best in the industry, but if your employees aren't committed to delivering it well, your company will fail.

IN POLITICS STUPIDITY
IS NOT A HANDICAP.

Napoleon Bonaparte

Strategic alignment

Strategy

How?

Strategy - in the context of "strategic alignment" - is the "how". The key question we need to ask before we can take any action to implement a strategic vision is, "How should we do that"

The big picture

The "big picture" of what you are trying to achieve combined with a high-level statement of how you are going to achieve it (by being low cost, increasing distribution while managing cash) is your "strategy"

Strategic alignment

Activity alignment

Research suggests that having a strategy has no real effect on the performance of your business. It's aligning your activities to your strategies that makes the difference

Strategic goals

The "how" statements lead you to strategic goals - the specific targets you have to hit to achieve your vision/mission.
- Reduce costs X%
- Improve cash flow Y%
- Increase distribution Z%

Want a cup of coffee?

Deciding you want a cup of coffee (your strategy) is not the same as getting up and making a cup of coffee (aligning your actions to your strategy)

z

It's the process of aligning an organization's decisions and actions such that they support the achievement of strategic goals. Also means STOP doing unaligned actions to strategy.

The importance of strategic alignment

Impact on performance

One study found that the level of strategic alignment of an organization explains up to 80% of the difference in performance between organizations. This is a quite startling result

Buy-in is also important

Another study found that 51% of the difference in organizations' performance can be explained by strategic alignment and another 38% can be explained by the level of consensus / buy-in

IT alignment is important

A 3rd study shows that **18%** of the difference between the overall performance of organizations is explained by the level of strategic alignment between business goals and the activities by the IT group

Strategic goals

Identify your goals

So take a look at your major projects and ask, "What are the business goals of this project?" - this will give you a good initial list of strategic goals. Also KPIs can be used to figure out what are the strategic goals

Assess goal importance

Not all goals are equal. Key stakeholders are unlikely to agree on importance of goals. So there needs to be a common "set of rules" that can guide decisions & actions to ensure goals are aligned & they are supported by everyone

Weighted map

Now you have a weighted map of your top level goals that clearly shows what's most important, you can share them with your team. The wider you share your goals, the more thoroughly your team understands what and why

Strategic planning

Strategic planning

Strategic planning is the process of defining strategy and turning it into a tactical plan.

Strategic planning

Strategic planning is the process of defining strategy and then cascading it down through the organization. It happens at all levels in the organization

Strategic planning done well

Strategic planning builds strategic alignment into everything you do as an organization

The measures of strategic alignment

Strategic alignment is not a tick box

Measuring strategic alignment is not simply a check box task as often the reply is YES

Strategic alignment assumptions

Assuming senior management can judge how to measure strategic alignment vs. staff

Contribution is key

What's the contribution X makes to your various strategic goals (projects, initiatives, new factory)

Project strategic alignment

20% of projects have little contribution

According to research by the PMI, 20% of projects in your portfolio contribute so little to strategic goals that they should be stopped

AHP and DEA methods

Out of 100 methods, only two methods are suitable for picking projects AHP & DEA

26 Steps to a completive strategy

You must define specific goals and objectives that are a direct outcome and reflection of your company's vision and mission while building a competitive strategy. Three factors must be kept in mind while implementing an effective competitive strategy in business today. You must continue to innovate your product or service, build consumer loyalty, and outperform or keep market share from your competitors.

A company's competitive advantage is the advantage it has over its competitors. This can be accomplished by providing clients with better and more valuable services. Consumer curiosity is piqued when products or services are advertised at cheaper prices or of higher quality. These one-of-a-kind items or services are well-known among target markets. This is the reason for customer loyalty to a brand, or why they prefer one product or service over another.

When a company offers the same products and services as its competitors, but at a lower price, it is said to have a cost advantage. When a company provides superior products and services than its competitors, it has a differentiation advantage. Price, location, quality, selection, speed, turnaround, and service are the six competitive advantage factors.

A firm's goal is to establish a defensive position in a certain industry while also providing a higher return on investment (Return on Investment). Establishing a competitive edge can be accomplished in three ways: Differentiation, cost leadership, and a laser-like focus (Cost-focus and Differentiation-focus). When there is fierce price competition, the service is a commodity available from many vendors, differentiation is difficult to achieve, the service application is standardized, switching costs are low, buyers have bargaining power, and new entrants use low cost to build their customer base, a low-cost strategy works best.

OUR LIBERTY DEPENDS ON THE
FREEDOM OF THE PRESS, AND
THAT CANNOT BE LIMITED
WITHOUT BEING LOST.

Thomas Jefferson

Steps to a completive strategy

Key questions

- **Current Issues:** Where are the ASIS organizational problems?
- **"TOBE" policies:** What policies to define to get organization to the "TO BE" state
- **Customers:** How to bring customers closer to the business?
- **Market:** What's the buying habits & behaviors of the customers?
- **Target state:** Where does the business want to be in the market?
- **Success measures:** How to measure strategy success?
- **Growth:** How to identify opportunities for growth & innovation?
- **Opportunities:** How best to leverage new opportunities?
- **Best in class:** What does the business do best in?
- **Objectives:** What are the growth and financial objectives?
- **Options:** What are the strategic business opportunities?
- **Direction:** Where is the company headed?
- **Leadership:** Is there leadership commitment for the strategy?
- **Events:** What are the political, economic, social and tech events that could impact the business?

Business objectives

- **Financials:** To increase earnings?
- **Market share:** To increase market share?
- **Customers:** To improve customer perception / retention?
- **Costs:** To attain lower operational costs?
- **Services:** To lead in products & services?
- **Technology:** To achieve superiority using technology innovation?

Situation analysis

- **Internal Organization matters:**
  - What is the organization's internal situation?
  - What are business strengths and weaknesses?
  - What are the capability gaps in the organization?
- **Operational processes:** How to transform operational processes to keep pace with the change of customer needs and behaviors?
- **External factors:**
  - What are the opportunities?
  - What are the threats?
  - What are the success factors?
- **Technology platforms:** What are the right technology platforms / development methodologies / security to deliver digital business scale, speed and flexibility?
- **Employee experience:** How to attract and retain talent within organization?-
- **Marketing:** What is the most effective marketing activities?
- **Data driven decision making:**
  - How to improve use of data driven decision making?
  - Does data support the business strategic needs?
- **Architectures:** Is the business architecture aligned with the technology / security architecture?
- **Workflows:** How to build strategic business process workflows that are automated, intelligent and efficient?
- **Existing programs and projects:** Are existing initiatives being reviewed for alignment with strategic objectives and if not, stopped?
- **Continuous change:** How to foster a culture of continuous improvement?

Competition analysis

- **Competition:**
  - What are the competitors doing?
  - Who uses identical technological approaches?
- **Competitors strategies:**
  - What are the current strategies of competitors?
  - What are the strengths and weaknesses of each competitor?
- **Digital competitors:** Understand the best approach and activities on how to take on digital competitors.
- **Competitive advantage:** How to create competitive advantages and deliver them in the form of technology solutions that increases efficiency and brings the customer closer to the business?

27 A lean competitive strategy

Companies are continuously looking for ways to get an advantage over their competitors in today's competitive global economy. By cutting back and focusing on the essentials, a lean strategy can help a company do more with less and increase efficiency. It can assist in identifying underutilized resources and reallocating them to activities that will benefit the company.

Companies must constantly improve the weaker elements of their business and innovate to generate new or improved products to compete in a crowded marketplace. The lean strategy focuses on revisiting all processes regularly to improve them and help the company progress and grow. As a result, you'll be in a great position to compete with other companies.

Lean is a collection of principles that can have a large-scale impact across an organization, improving business results and competitiveness.

The goal of a lean approach is to accomplish tasks more productively and cost-effectively than the competition. It's a continuous process that examines how a company performs and then proposes adjustments to reduce waste, boost productivity, and improve overall customer value. Production, product development, customer service, inventory management, cost savings, and other aspects of a firm can all benefit from lean.

Lean helps the company target and enhance its customer service operations by eliminating inefficient procedures like customer wait times and call transfers and concentrating on the things that bring value. Businesses can achieve high-quality results for their consumers while lowering operating expenses by embracing lean-to eliminate inefficient procedures and streamline their approach.

ALWAYS RESPECT YOUR SUPERIORS; IF YOU HAVE ANY.

Mark Twain

A lean competitive strategy

A competitive edge

Competitive edge comes from customer value
Competitive edge come from value a business is able to create to their customers

Customers will pay for value
Customers are willing to pay for value & superior value stems from offering lower prices than the competitors

Ways to achieve a competitive edge

Find your purpose in business
When a business finds its why, it is connected to a purpose that drives its customers to buy their products. The story of a business is a link to its core principles

Ask your customers
The loyal customers of a business are a goldmine of information about how a company is perceived and what's making them buy from you instead of someone else

Understand your brand
Use a brand wheel to make a distillation of company's brand strategy by breaking it down into five categories: attributes, benefits, values, personality, and essence

Traditional strategies

For a business to gain & maintain a competitive edge, it needs to continually innovate.

Differentiation strategy
Branding used method to differentiate where a business creates a status distinct & apart from other businesses in the same market

Cost leadership strategy
Competitive pricing is selecting strategic price points to best take advantage of a product based market relative to competition

Operational effectiveness
This strategy allows a firm to develop products at a faster pace than competitors

Technology based strategy
A business can leverage IT as a competitive advantage in value activities (cost & differentiation

Innovation strategy
A business may move ahead of the competition by doing things in new & different ways to gain a competitive edge over other businesses

Adaptability based strategy
Some companies use adaptability to keep products relevant, valuable & maintain its competitive edge

Information based strategy
Businesses can create a competitive edge using data to outperform the competition

Ways for a company to become lean

Value to customers
A lean strategy is about offering value to customers

Focus on the value creation process
The main goal of a lean strategy is to offer value to customers with more focus on the value creation process

Focus on flow
To increase the creation of value, a lean strategy focuses on flow of products as wanted by customers

Optimise the whole
Optimize the Whole is a key part of Lean strategy that ensures that all of the moving parts are aligned so that they are made best use with limited resources

Build quality into the system
Create a system that is built for growth, where the system is error-proof by standardizing and automating it with a focus on innovation and continuous improvement

Manage flow by limiting work in progress
Staff need to work in a space that permits them to focus & they can only deliver fast if flow is managed by limiting work in process (WIP) at the organizational level

Defer commitment
A key aspect of giving customers what they want is making decisions based on real, customer-driven data

Respect people
Respect for people creates a work place where best ideas are heard, where good staff is retained, & leaders can understand needs of staff & customers

Create knowledge
This lean principle gives firms the challenge of continuously improving processes, to reach the level of speed and desired growth

Eliminate waste
Waste, in Lean is defined as anything that does not add value to the customer, would not willingly pay for

Knowhow waste

- Task switching
- Unnecessary features
- Lengthy feedback loops
- Premature planning
- Complex decision making
- Technical debt

Ways to reduce knowledge work waste

Make waste visible
Staff experience lots waste in terms of delays

Make tacit knowledge explicit
Many tasks can be standardised and by using tacit knowledge it can be improved

Solve problem consistently
A systematic approach to problem solving can speed up processes

Review the structure of every job
Managers regularly assess their team members tasks, and the time spent on each task

Ask the 5 whys
Why am I at this meeting? Why am I filling out this report?

Small bits of waste that add up to big waste
E-mail clutter because of cc'd all unnecessarily? Waiting time to start meetings owing to late people?

28 Strategy and its deployment

Any type of organizational improvement in which solutions come from the individuals closest to the problem is referred to as strategy deployment. The name is derived from the Japanese term Hoshin Kanri, which translates to "Direction Management," implying both setting and steering toward a goal. Developing a successful competitive strategy is a result of a combination of elements that address crucial features of the current situation.

The ability of a corporation to develop a competitive edge based on the outcomes of its actions determines its success and profitability. A smart strategy defines which activities to prioritize and how to prioritize them to give the most value to clients while also gaining a competitive advantage over competitors. The overall strategy analysis and the positioning analysis are used to choose a competitive strategy.

The organizational focus determines whether this study uses an industrial or market approach. Focusing on and arranging various tasks might provide a competitive advantage (backward, forward or horizontal linkages, vertical integration). Competitive advantage should be long-term, not only for a short period.

The danger is that if a company concentrates on the few areas where it excels and ignores its flaws, it may lose its competitive edge. When a company's environment changes and it is unable to adjust to new circumstances in time to maintain market share, a strategy failure occurs.

When it comes to strategy, it's all about making decisions, and you can't do everything. A smart plan can help you focus your efforts on the activities that will provide the most value, allowing you to avoid wasting time on non-essential tasks. The steps you'll take to achieve the aims and objectives defined by your management are referred to as strategies.

THOSE WHO STAND FOR
NOTHING FALL FOR
EVERYTHING.

Alexander Hamilton

Strategy and its deployment

Strategy questions

Current problems	Best in class	Growth	Market goals	Growth & financial objectives	Market	Policies	Leadership	Opportunities	Measures	Customers
Where are the current organizational issues?	What does the business do best in class?	The opportunities for growth & innovation?	What are the business market goals?	What are the growth and financial objectives?	What's customers buying habits & behaviors?	What policies to define to get to "TO BE" state	Is there leadership commitment for strategy?	How best to leverage new market opportunities, the strategic / tactical business opportunities?	How to measure strategy success?	How to bring customers closer to business?

Business objectives

- Increase earnings
- Increase market share
- Improve customer perception
- Lower operating costs
- Lead in products & services
- use technology innovation

Strategy deployment

Translate strategy — Successful companies tend to have a method to translate strategy into operative terms (KPIs) & evaluate it daily

Communicate strategy — Many successful organizations have a formal mechanism to communicate strategy to their staff

Manage strategy — Most successful companies use a formal process to manage strategy to outperform their peers

Barriers to successful strategy deployment

	Visibility of strategic direction	Company's value proposition	Team alignment with strategy
Employee Awareness	Lack of visibility to the organization's strategic vision	Lack of understanding of the company's value delivery	Lack of in strategy topics in weekly team meetings
	Reliable data	Compensation alignment	Corporate budget alignment
Change execution	Lack of reliable data	Lack of alignment with strategy & staff payments	Lack of links with corporate budget & strategic goals
	Change tools	Visibility of risk	Knowledge management
	Lack of tools to track change actions	Lack of transparency into areas of risk	Lack of accessibility to a central archive of issue & best practices
	Monitoring performance		
Performance governance	Lack of tools to monitor and benchmark performance		

Desired strategy deployment goals

More visibility of performance — Improved Top-down visibility into performance governance

Increased confidence — Increased confidence that expectations and annual goals agreed and achieved

Improved cost benefits analysis on CI opportunities — Elaborated cost & benefits analysis on business improvement opportunities

Defined roles and responsibilities — Clearly defined roles and responsibilities (RACI). Manage up & be efficient in communicating where support is required

Real time engagement and involvement — Real time involvement in operational activities & issues requiring tactical decision making

improved visibility of risk — Increased insight to when annual and breakthrough targets are at risk

Improved reporting of annual goals and KPIs — Annual goals and KPIs measured and reported with greater frequency and accuracy

Real time feedback to staff — Coach and evaluate staff with electronic, real-time feedback. Thank and endorse your employees

Share ideas for continuous improvement — Share ideas on continuous improvement activities and communicate and celebrate improvement success

Visibility of staff talent — Enhanced visibility into staff talent & innovation opportunities given by staff

29 Develop business capabilities

The APQC Process Classification Framework is an open standard that was created to reflect 21st-century process management. Its goal is to assist organizations in developing robust processes that effectively service customers and other external stakeholders, deliver value through risk-appropriate controls, and do it as quickly as feasible. This process classification framework (PCF) is a method for classifying processes into a common taxonomy that can be used for benchmarking and process improvement. The PCF from APQC contains hundreds of processes and metrics, allowing for a common framework of business processes and metrics.

The Process Classification Framework® is a comprehensive tool that provides precise, industry-agnostic descriptions of a company's business processes and provides a common language for defining and conveying capabilities, operations, and responsibilities. It is the initial step in establishing a benchmarking program for a company.

Create a list of business capabilities and identify the success criteria and supporting processes for each capability using the Process Capability Assessment tool.

First, determine each Business Capability before constructing a Business Capability Model, then arrange them together to create a logical framework. Then further breakdown each Business Capability to discover specific components of the capability that are distinct, well-bounded, and deserve to be highlighted on their own. Defining the supporting components of a business capability (roles, processes, information, and tools) gives those components a business context. Creating a business capacity model for the company provides a better knowledge of the company's operations. A bank's risk management or credit department management are examples of capabilities; other skills include sales pipeline management, information security management, and pricing.

TIME STAYS LONG ENOUGH FOR
ANYONE WHO WILL USE IT.

Leonardo da Vinci

Develop business capabilities

Manage business processes

Establish process management governance
- Define governance approach
- Establish process tools & templates
- Assign & support process ownership
- Perform process governance activities

Define process framework
- Establish and maintain process framework
- Identify cross-functional processes

Define processes
- Scope and analyse processes
- Identify published best practices
- Document processes
- Publish processes

Manage process performance
- Provide process training
- Support process execution
- Measure and report process performance
- Identify additional metrics

Improve processes
- Identify and select improvement opportunities
- Manage improvement projects
- Perform continuous improvement activities

Manage portfolio, programs & projects

Manage portfolio
- Establish portfolio strategy
- Define portfolio governance
- Monitor and control portfolio

Manage programs
- Establish program approach
- Manage program stakeholders
- Manage program execution
- Report program performance

Manage projects
- Establish project scope, project goals, resources
- Assess culture & readiness for PM approach
- Identify PM methodologies
- Business case & funding
- Develop project measures

Develop project plans
- Define roles and resources
- Identify IT requirements
- Create training and comms plans
- Design reward approaches
- Design & plan launch of project
- Deploy project

Execute and close projects
- Evaluate impact of PM strategy and projects on measures
- Report the status of project
- Manage project scope
- Realign PM strategy and approaches
- Review and report project performance
- Close projects

Manage enterprise quality

Establish quality requirements
- Define critical-to-quality characteristics
- Define preventive quality activities
- Develop quality controls
- Define plan & measurement methods
- Define required competencies
- Prove capability for compliance
- Finalise quality plan
- Define steps for controls

Manage non-conformance
- Assess potential impact
- Determine action(s)
- Identify root cause(s)
- Take corrective or preventative action
- Close non-conformance

Evaluate performance requirements
- Test against quality plan
- Conduct test and collect data
- Record result(s)
- Determine disposition of result(s)
- Assess results of tests
- Assess sample significance
- Summarise result(s)
- Recommend actions & next steps

Implement enterprise quality management system (EQMS)
- Define the quality strategy
- Plan the EQMS scope, targets & goals
- Identify EQMS processes and metrics
- Develop and document EQMS standards, & metrics
- Assess the EQMS performance
- Create capability for EQMS improvement(s)
- Reward quality excellence
- Create and maintain quality partnerships
- Maintain talent capabilities
- Incorporate EQMS messaging into comms channels
- Assure independent EQMS management access to appropriate authority in the organization
- Transfer proven EQMS methods

30 Key performance indicators

A set of quantifiable statistics used to judge a company's overall long-term performance is referred to as key performance indicators (KPIs). KPIs are used to determine a company's strategic, financial, and operational accomplishments, especially when compared to those of other companies in the same industry. When creating an effective program plan, it is critical to have a clear understanding of the organization's goals and objectives. Check that programs are aligned with the organization's goals, and if they aren't, both the goals and the program should be evaluated. The aims of the organization can be communicated in a variety of ways. Displaying the organization's goal, vision, and/or values around key performance metrics is one method (KPIs).

Key performance indicators (KPIs) are a method of evaluating the performance of organisations, business units, divisions, departments, and people regularly. As a result, KPIs are frequently established in an intelligible, meaningful, and measurable manner.

They are rarely defined in such a way that their achievement is inhibited by variables that the organisations or individuals in charge view as uncontrollable.. Organizations typically overlook such KPIs; instead, KPIs should adhere to the SMART criteria This means the measure has a specific purpose for the business, it is measurable to truly determine the KPIs value, the defined norms must be achievable, the improvement of a KPI must be relevant to the organization's success, and it must finally be time phased, which means the value or outcomes are displayed for a predetermined and relevant period. KPIs are linked to goal values to be evaluated, allowing the value of the measure to be appraised as meeting or not meeting expectations.

Without a strategy, you won't be able to achieve your objectives. The planning of KPIs in each area of your firm, from fully established to emerging, is the first step in the KPIs program. To assist you in the planning process, use the KPIs process flow diagram. Customer satisfaction, internal process quality, employee satisfaction, financial performance, and customer acquisition cost are examples of KPIs.

WORRY IS THE INTEREST PAID BY THOSE WHO BORROW TROUBLE.

George Washington

Key performance indicators (1)

The KPIs process

Business objectives	Current performance	Set KPIs targets	Stakeholders	Review progress
Review business objectives	Analyse current performance	Set short & long term KPIs targets	Review KPIs with stakeholders	Review progress & change is needed

KPIs categorisation

Quantitative facts
Quantitative facts without distortion from personal feelings, prejudices, or interpretations presented with a specific value – objective - preferably numeric measured against a standard.

Qualitative values
Qualitative values based on or influenced by personal feelings, tastes, or opinions and presented as any numeric or textual value that represents an interpretation of these elements.

Key questions

Desired outcome	Outcome importance	Measuring progress	KPIs Responsibility
What is the desired outcome?	Why this outcome important?	How will progress be measured?	Who is responsible for the outcome?
KPIs outcome influence How can the KPIs outcome be influenced?	**KPIs outcome achievement** How will it be known if KPI is achieved?	**KPIs review frequency** How often will KPIs progress be reviewed?	**KPIs smart criteria** Is there SMART criteria to evaluate KPIs performance?

Points of measurement

Input	Output	Activity
Input indicates inputs required of an activity to produce an output	Output captures the outcome or results of an activity	Activity indicates the transformation produced by an activity
Mechanism Mechanism is something that enables an activity to work	**Control** Something that controls the activity's production via. compliance	**Time** Time indicates a temporal element of the activity

KPIs indicators

Pre-defined business process	Business process requirements	Quantitative /Qualitative measurements of results
Having a pre-defined business process	Have requirements for the business processes	Having a quantitative / qualitative metric of the results

Investigating variance: Investigating variances and tweaking processes or resources to achieve short-term goals

Smart KPIs

Specific	Measurable	Achievable	Relevant	Time
Specific aim for the business	Measurable to really get a value of the KPIs	The defined norms have to be achievable	KPIs are relevant to the company success	KPIs must be time phased

OKR framework

Objectives and key results (OKR) is a goal-setting framework that helps organizations define goals and then track the outcome. The framework helps organizations establish far-reaching goals in days instead of months

The difference between KPI and OKR goals
KPIs goals are typically obtainable and represent the output of a process or project already in place, while OKR goals are somewhat more aggressive and ambitious

Keep it simple	Cascade goals	Be wary of goals	Mini goals
Focus on goals that can be achieved in a given time frame	To ensure staff see how their jobs are contributing to a company's success	Goals need to be attainable and challenging at the same time	Create mini goals within your key results.

Celebrate
Reward & recognize staff when a milestone met

KPIs best practices

Be specific	Narrow focus on KPIs	Make it measurable	KPIs aligned to goals
Brainstorm different ways to reach the results	Define KPIs list to avoid data overload	Key results need to have a unit of measurement	Ensure KPIs aligned with business goals
		Measurable Ensure KPIs are achievable	

Use KPIs smarter practice
Specific, Measurable, Attainable, Relevant, Time, Evaluate, Re-evaluate

Key performance indicators (2)

Accounts KPIs

- **Overdue invoices** — Percentage of overdue invoices
- **Advance purchase orders** — Percentage of purchase orders raised in advance
- **Retrospective POs** — Number of retrospectively raised purchase orders
- **Duplicate payments** — Number of duplicate payments
- **Report quality** — Finance report error rate
- **Cycle time** — Average cycle time of workflow

Marketing and sales KPIs

- **Profitability** — Profitability of customers /
- **Potential customers** — Demographic analysis of people as potential customers
- **Revenue generated** — Revenue generated by segments of the customer population
- **Balances** — Outstanding balances held by segments of customers
- **Bad debts** — Collection of bad debts from customers
- **New customers** — New customer acquisition

Manufacturing KPIs

- **Equipment effectiveness** — OEE (measure of how well a manufacturing operation is utilised = availability x performance x quality
- **Machine availability** — Availability = run time / total time (% production time running)
- **Performance** — Performance = total count / target counter (% of total parts produced on a machine)
- **Quality** — Quality = good count / total count (% good parts out of the total parts produced on the machine

Professional KPIs

- **Utilisation rate** — The % of time employees spend generating revenue
- **Project profitability** — The difference of the revenue generated versus the delivery cost of work
- **Project success rate** — The percentage of projects delivered on time and under budget

HR KPIs

- Employee turnover
- Employee performance indicators
- Cross functional team analysis

System KPIs

- Availability / uptime
- Mean time between failure
- Mean time to repair
- Unplanned availability
- Average time to repair

Project execution KPIs

- Earned value
- Cost variance
- Schedule variance
- Estimate to complete
- Resources spent / month
- Money spent / month
- Planned spend / month
- planned resources / month
- Average time to delivery
- Tasks / staff
- Project overhead / ROI
- Planned delivery date vs. actual

SCM processes

Main supplier chain management KPIs will detail the following processes:

- Sales forecasts
- inventory
- Procurement
- Warehousing
- Transportation
- Product reuse

Supply chain management

Any business, regardless of size, can better manage supplier performance with the help of KPIs robust capabilities, which includes:

- **Automated approval** — Automated entry and approval functions
- **On demand real time scorecard** — On-demand, real-time scorecard measures
- **Single data repository** — Single data repository to eliminate inefficiencies & maintain consistency
- **Advanced workflow** — Advanced workflow approval process to ensure consistency
- **Flexible data input models** — Flexible data-input modes and real-time graphical performance display
- **Rework** — Rework on procured inventory
- **Documents** — Customized cost savings documentation
- **Simplified set up procedures** — Simplified setup procedures to eliminate dependence upon IT resources

31 Lean six sigma

Lean Six Sigma is a performance improvement strategy that depends on a collaborative team effort to eliminate waste and reduce variance. To remove the eight types of waste, it blends lean manufacturing/lean enterprise and Six Sigma. Lean Six Sigma is a management strategy that combines Lean and Six Sigma. Six Sigma focuses on increasing process output quality by detecting and removing the sources of defects (errors) and limiting variability in (manufacturing and business) processes, while Lean focuses on eliminating the eight types of waste ("Muda"). The DMAIC phases are used in Lean Six Sigma, just as they are in Six Sigma. The five steps of Lean Six Sigma are designed to pinpoint the source of inefficiencies and can be applied to any process, product, or service that has a lot of data or measurable qualities. Fujio Cho defines waste (Muda) as "everything else than the bare minimum of equipment, materials, parts, space, and labour time required to add value to the product."

Different types of waste have been defined using a "downtime" mnemonic:

- **Defects:** A flaw in a product that renders it inappropriate for use, necessitating the product's scrapping or rework, both of which cost the company time and money

- **Overproduction**: When a product is produced in excess or before it is required, it is referred to as overproduction.

- **Waiting:** Waiting refers to delays in process phases and is divided into two categories: material and equipment waiting, and idle equipment waiting.

- **Non-Used Talent:** This term alludes to the squandering of human potential and ability. When management is separated from employees, employees are unable to provide feedback and recommendations to managers to improve the process flow, and production suffers as a result.

- **Transportation:** Transportation refers to the movement of materials, products, people, equipment, and tools that is either unneeded or excessive.

- **Inventory:** Unprocessed extra items and commodities are referred to as inventory.

- **Motion:** People who move around unnecessarily. Excessive movement consumes time and puts you at risk of harm.

- **Extra-processing:** Doing more effort than is required or necessary to finish a task is referred to as extra-processing.

PAINTING IS SILENT POETRY,
AND POETRY IS PAINTING
THAT SPEAKS.

Plutarch

Lean six sigma

Lean
A methodology for increasing process speed & improving efficiency through waste reduction | The change in culture & mindset of an organization with Lean maximises efficiency & increases profitability

Lean is **not** a business strategy | Lean is **not** only for manufacturing firms | Lean is **not** about people reductions | Lean is **not** only about the tools

Lean benefits

Profitability
A result o removing waste & improving quality of production

Simplified processes
Simple processes mean less waste, reduced time, leading to a decrease in overhead costs

Decrease in errors
With simple processes and detailed looks at causes of errors

Employee performance
Increased employee motivation from empowerment for ideas

Value to customer
Lean results in better quality, less errors, more client satisfaction

Lean principles

Customer
Focus on customer

The value stream
Understand how work gets done

Process flow
Manage, improve flow

Remove waste
Remove Non-Value-Add steps

Reduce variation
Manage by fact

Involve people
In lean process

Improvement
Be systematic

Why lean fails

Lack of exec support | Wrong deployment | Incorrect Project Selection | Choosing a wrong process | Inappropriate team members

Lack of process owner support | Incorrect scope | Incorrect training | Incorrect Measurement System | Incorrect Implementation

Process definition

Management processes (Governance) | **Core processes (Important to the customer)** | **Support processes**

| Strategy | Governance | Planning | Contracts | Customers | Assembly | Testing | Recruiting | Production | Accounts |

"5S"

5S can be applied on all processes - organise what is needed, where it is needed, in the needed quantities

Sort
Focus on the elimination of any unnecessary clutter

Straighten
Create workspace that is organized uncluttered and easily navigable

Shine
This next step is to properly and clean the work area every day

Standardise
It's time to standardize these new practices with employees involved

Sustain
Remain disciplined enough to sustain the positive changes made previously

7 wastes of lean

Transport
Movement of parts more than needed

Inventory
Stock of most anything is waste

Motion
Non-added value movement of people / tools

Waiting
Wait time is idle time (people, machines, info or material)

Over production
Producing more than is demanded or needed

Over processing
Putting in more work than needed for client's reeds

Defects
Rework & defects take time, people, capacity

The path to lean

Define value
Define value from client's view & express value in a product terms

Data driven decisions
Data allows you to objectively identify and select the best ideas

Map
Map all of he steps that bring a service to the customer

Maximize flow
Make the remaining steps in the value stream flow (eliminate barriers)

Create pull
Let customer pull products as needed, eliminating the need for a sales forecast

Involve the owners
Involve the owner of process being worked on, then owner will own change

Continuously improve
There is no end to process of reducing effort, time, space, cost, and mistakes

Lean best practices

Leadership
Make commitment to change & understand meaning of lean

Think before action
Don't confuse action with success, define the issue & solution

Align lean with strategy
Align lean program with strategy with regular progress reviews

Minimise variations
Variations can often cause more damage than their level

Set expectations
Most journeys starts with ardour, then hits issues before it recovers

Empowerment & engagement
Lean is about empowered employees & that all employees are engaged at all levels

Set stretch goals
Lean is for organizations who want to improve efficiency by leaps and bounds.

Lean is continuous
Lean is about continuous improvement not one-off program approach

32   What types of value do you offer?

Providing valuable products and services to your customers can boost sales, increase customer loyalty, and improve the reputation of your company. Consumers typically seek value in the form of money and time. Providing helpful products and services that customers think are worthy of their time, energy, and money is what creating value for customers entails. A product's or service's perceived benefits must outweigh its cost for buyers to see it as valuable. Creating value entails maximizing advantages while staying within a reasonable price range. The two main components of consumer value are benefits and cost. Quality, popularity, accessibility, convenience, and longevity are all possible advantages. Customers will value your product or service more if you increase the benefits without increasing the price.

Brands, on the other hand, can provide psychological, aesthetic, and societal value. What kind of value do you provide? What is your definition of value? Are you able to quantify it?

What are the true costs of your products and services to customers? Surprisingly few business market suppliers can answer those inquiries.

In layman's terms, value refers to the amount of money that something is worth (cash, importance). The economy relies on a diverse range of goods and services. Consumers perceive different sorts of value depending on the trade-offs they make between price, performance, quality, and service-related aspects. Value can also refer to a consumer's impression of a product or service that is closely related to determining customer happiness and loyalty. Customers are more likely to purchase from companies that share their principles and basic beliefs.

**TO LOVE BEAUTY IS TO
SEE LIGHT.**

Victor Hugo

What types of value do you offer?

Business value principles
- **Customer & leadership:** Improve value from client feedback. Strategies, processes & resources are aligned for customer value
- **Engagement:** Staff are engaged to improve the firm where success is recognised
- **Process:** Performance manages processes for coherent value management system
- **Improvement:** improvement focus to maintain performance & to spot new ideas
- **Decisions:** Decisions are data driven s to identify facts, analyse data & impacts
- **Relationships:** Poor relations with partners can impact success

Value proposition
- **A better life:** How does product make life better?
- **Product:** Why product created?
- **Customer:** What value in client mind?
- **Generation:** How is value of put in product?
- **Audience:** Who is the target audience for the product?
- **Value type:** What pain points is the product addressing?
- **Solution:** How does product remedy audiences pain?

Value management process
- **Framing:** Setting the goals for a value study
- **Data gathering:** Where data is defined & collected
- **Analysis:** Looks at the parts & decide what is performed
- **Creative:** Look to find improvements
- **Judgement:** Look at results to filter out the potential ideas
- **Approvals:** Develop ideas to for approval
- **Execution:** Ideas executed

Bus. principles
Consistency | Honesty | Efficiency | Innovation | Creativity | Passion | Reliability | Dependability

Marketing values
- **Functional value:** What the solution offers in customer value
- **Monetary value:** The cost of an offering's & perceived worth with trade-off to other values
- **Social value:** The scale of owning or using a product / service that lets someone connect to others
- **Psychological value:** The extent of owning or using a product that lets someone feel better

Business value
Fixtures | Utility | Monetary assets | Stakeholder equity | Brand recognition | Goodwill | Public benefits | Trademarks

Value measures
Revenue | Profits | Brand | Market share | Customer loyalty | Customer retention | Customer satisfaction | Share of wallet

Business value steps
- **Vision:** Understand Vision
- **Business value:** Project has clear value
- **Promote business value:** Promote vision & business value to team, partners and customers
- **Measure business value:** Processes & tools to measure business value

Project business value
- **To deliver business value:** Project must have a clear objective
- **Aligned to business strategy and objectives:** A project to deliver business value must be aligned to the business goals
- **Aligned with stakeholders:** A project to deliver business value must have stakeholder support

Tech bus. value
Security | Agility | Availability | Reliability | Functionality | Performance

Process maps
- **SIPOC:** Supplier –Inputs –Process –Outputs –Customer
- **High level process map:** Shows how the process works in a few steps
- **Swimlane map:** This map splits steps into lanes by person activity
- **Value stream map:** Show ASIS process for process improvement

Process value
- **Value added step:** The steps to add something to a product for which the customer is willing to pay
- **Non added value step but not necessary:** Process steps that do not add value, but are necessary to make the product or service happen
- **Non added value steps (waste):** These steps resources are expended, delays occur, and no value is added to the product or service (delays, inventory)

33 Business process mapping

The activities involved in establishing what a business entity performs, who is responsible, to what standard a business process should be accomplished, and how the success of a business process can be measured are referred to as business process mapping. The primary goal of business process mapping is to help firms become more efficient. Outside firms can look at a clear and precise business process map or diagram to see if any changes can be made to the current process. Business process mapping takes a specific goal and helps measure and compare it to the organization's overall goals to ensure that all processes are in line with the company's values and capabilities. The activity of business process mapping is looking at the tasks that are performed in a company and then visualizing them on a diagram. To increase the quality of the end-to-end business process, business process mapping can also be used to model hypothetical future processes. Implementing a procedure without first planning it out is a common blunder. This can be accomplished by generating a business process map.

This is a detailed written map of the many phases for each step in your operations, with each step stated in a simple sequence form that you may use to do your tasks more quickly.

Process mapping's key steps in process improvement are:

1. Identify the process's objectives, scope, players, and work areas.

2. Gather process facts (what, who, where, and when) from the people who perform the work.

3. Convert information into a process map using process mapping.

4. Analyse the map by questioning each step (what-why? who-why? where-why? when-why? how-why?)

5. Create/implement new methods - reduce redundant tasks, combine processes, reorder stages, and add new phases as needed.

6. Manage the process - keep a process map in the library, review it regularly, and keep an eye on it for changes.

MY POWERS ARE ORDINARY. ONLY MY
APPLICATION BRINGS ME SUCCESS.

Isaac Newton

Business process mapping

Process framework

- **Best practices** — Identify process best practices
- **"TOBE" processes** — Implement "TOBE" processes
- **Map "AS IS" processes** — Map out "ASIS" process as it happens now
- **Review "AS IS" process** — Analyse & check "ASIS" process
- **"TOBE" processes** — Create future "TOBE" process
- **Review "TOBE" process** — Review "TOBE" process before implementation
- **Target state** — All current processes mapped out & implement new "TOBE" processes
- **Review "TOBE" process** — Review "TOBE" process after implementation for continuous improvement

Mapping steps

- **High level diagram** — Start with a high level flow diagram
- **Start & end of each sub-process** — Define the start and end of each sub-process
- **Inputs & outputs** — Define key inputs and outputs
- **Process & technology** — Identify process & technology opportunities
- **Review accuracy** — Review & verify process accuracy

Process mapping requirements

- **Key responsibilities for process** — Determine key responsibilities for the processes
- **Internal and external recipients** — Identify recipients of each activity
- **Record all activities** — Record key activities in each process area
- **Main source of data** — Determine main source of data input for each activity
- **Existing KPIs** — Record any existing KPIs for processes
- **Key volumes** — Identify key volumes for activities
- **Key deliverables** — Identify key deliverables of each activity

Process mapping questions

- **Customers** — Who are process customers?
- **How and why** — How is it done & why is it done?
- **Problems** — What's frequency & impact?
- **Who does each activity?** — Who performs each activity?
- **Process decisions** — What decisions are made in the process?
- **Problem handling** — How are issues & problems handled?
- **Source of process** — What generates the process?
- **Sequence of activities** — What sequence of activities are done?
- **Process reviewers** — Who reviews process and when?
- **Forms & documents** — What forms & documents are used?
- **Process time** — How long does the process take?
- **Process outputs** — What's the outputs & where do they go?
- **Systems & files** — What systems & files are used?
- **Process problems** — What are the cause of problems?
- **Opportunities** — ID improvement opportunities?

Process maps

- System automation
- Continuous improvement
- Standards & compliance
- Organization design
- Change & transformation

Example online process mapping tool - Skore

- **Online mapping tool** — Skore is an online process mapping & analysis software for agile organizations
- **Digital first approach** — The digital approach means you focus on describing the flow of work without interruption of rewriting sticky notes
- **Good for rapid transformation change** — Deliver rapid transformational change, Designed for mapping at the speed of conversation'
- **Single integrated approach** — With Skore you create a single integrated model of your people, processes and technology show gaps and dependencies
- **Excellent for remote teams** — Engage through live online or face to face workshops, deliver instant insights & share easily
- **Defines what happens** — Skore defines the work that happens in the organization (business process) and it works in conjunction with Visio and lucid chart

Best practices

- **Map process ASIS** — Map the process as it happens
- **Organizational view** — Take process view across the organization
- **All stakeholders involved** — All stakeholders and SME's are involved in the design process
- **Define start and end** — Define start and end before any process mapping
- **High level view** — Start with a high level view of process

34 Root cause analysis

Root Cause Analysis (RCA) is being used by organisations all over the world to identify important problems and turn them into opportunities to enhance goods, services, and operations. Any successful business relies on its capacity to increase quality and customer happiness. Instead of blaming individuals or focusing on symptoms, the purpose of RCA is to precisely identify the root causes of all problems. The goal of RCA is to find the root of the problem and then build a solution that has fewer negative side effects.

Root Cause Analysis is a problem-solving technique for determining the source of errors or problems. It employs a method that entails a thorough examination of the problem's potential origins on three levels: immediate, underlying, and precipitating. It is a procedure for determining the true cause(s) of an issue, rather than a type of analysis or fault-finding.

The goal is to eradicate these core causes and, as a result, prevent the problem from recurring. In quality management, it is a step-by-step procedure. A basic RCA can be utilised to solve both little and huge, complex issues. Its goal is to keep the same problem from happening again.

What causes some products to fail? Manufacturers frequently blame users for product misuse, but it's only fair to inform them about the genuine cause when the product is defective. Root cause analysis (RCA) is a step-by-step problem-solving method for determining the root cause of a product's failure. The proper analysis of a customer's complaint allows the customer service department to determine what can be done to eliminate the cause of the defect or problem and prevent recurrence; it also allows the firm to enhance its quality of service. The RCA approach is critical for preventing and decreasing losses associated with an organization's services.

THE FUTURE DEPENDS ON
WHAT WE DO IN THE PRESENT.

Gandhi

Root cause analysis (1)

Key areas	Points to consider					
Roots cause analysis	**How and why** — RCA identifies how and why problems and issues occur. Identify what can be done to stop recurrence	**Areas of change** — RCA is used to identify areas for change and to develop options, which deliver better solutions	**Type of causes** — Something stopped working. Human – people done wrong action or did not do action. Firm system, process, not working	**Root cause analysis goals** — To focus on prevention, not blame. To identify changes that can be made in systems, which will reduce or remove the problem. What happened? Why did it happen? What to do to prevent problem again? How to know the change made a difference?	**Focus areas** — Focuses on system & process weaknesses, communication, environment, equipment, training, policies and processes	**Root cause uses** — Identify areas for change. Develop recommendations. Identify new solutions
Root cause analysis best practices	**Keep it simple** — Use short phrases and bullet points. Consider small changes that can make a difference	**Leadership** — The success of RCA initiatives depends upon visible leadership support and participation. Ensure full and active participation and commitment by key stakeholders to the RCA process and identified preventative actions	**Positive & creative** — Be positive, objective about solving problems with "no blame" attitude or finer pointing	**RCA effectiveness** — RCA actions will be measured via aligned metrics for effectiveness in preventing future issues	**RCA Facilitator** — Ensures a "no blame" approach. The team focus on solutions, not the problem. Provide training and consultation. Keeps the team on task to find root causes and effective actions for the issue. Ensure information is captured document	
Root cause analysis process	**1. Team** — Organize a small team of stakeholders and subject matter experts (SMEs).	**2. Define problem** — Create map of "What happened? What are the specific symptoms".	**3. Collect data** — What proof is that the problem exists? How long has the problem existed? What is the impact of the problem?	**4. find causes** — What order of events leads to the problem? What context for the problem to occur? What other problems occur?	**5. Root cause** — Use RCA tools, such as the 5 Why's and fishbone diagram to find causes.	**6. Create action plan and metrics** — Develop an aligned action plan to fix the problem. How will the solution be implemented? Who will be responsible for the solution and signoff? What are the risks of implementing the solution? How will be measured & comms
The 5 whys tool	**Purpose** — The purpose of this tool is to constantly ask WHY? Through the various layers of causes of a problem to determine the root cause	**Starting point** — Use the identified problem as the starting point of the root cause analysis process	**The problem** — Use brain-storming to identify main features of the problem. Analyse issues separately	**Problem causes** — Ask what is the cause of the original problem? Generate further and deeper reasons as to why the issue exists	**Map process** — Map the process on a flipchart or whiteboard. For each cause, ask what is the cause of the original problem? Map the process on a flipchart, until no more causes are identified, then you should have found the root of the problem	**The 5 whys** — The process normally requires FIVE (5) rounds of the question "WHY" to elicit the root of a problem, but, this is not cast in stone

Root cause analysis (2)

Fishbone diagrams

Purpose

A fishbone diagram is used to identify all of the contributing root causes likely to be causing a problem.

Cause category groups

Causes are usually grouped into these categories.
- People: Anyone involved with the process
- Methods: How the process is performed and the specific requirements for doing it
- Materials: Raw materials used to produce the final product
- Measurements: Data generated from the process, which are used to evaluate its quality
- Environment: The conditions: such as location, time, and culture in which the process operates

Marketing cause groups

- Product / Service
- Price
- Place
- Promotion
- People / Personnel
- Positioning
- Packaging

5 whys cause groups

- Who
- Where
- What
- When
- Why

The fishbone process

- Use a flipchart or whiteboard to get started
- Draw the "backbone" of the fish
- Write the problem to be solved as detailed as possible to the head of the fish (right-hand side of fishbone diagram)
- The next step is to decide how to categorize the causes
- Use "Post-It" notes to move causes to decide on categories for fishbone
- You can use the traditional cause categories or decide your own
- Brainstorm with team members to identify causes within the agreed cause category groupings

Kaizen

Purpose & goals

- A practice that focuses upon continuous improvement of processes, which can be continuously improve solutions identified by RCA
- Standardize an operation and activities
- Measure the operation
- Gauge measurements against requirements
- Innovate to meet requirements and increase productivity.
- Standardize the new, improved operations.
- Continue the cycle of process improvement

Kaizen 10 step process

1. Define the problem.
2. Document the current situation
3. Visualize the ideal situation
4. Define measurement targets
5. Brainstorm solutions to the problem
6. Develop KAIZEN plan.
7. Implement plan
8. Measure, record, and compare results to targets
9. Prepare summary documents
10. Create a short-term action plan

The 5 elements of kaizen

These are the FIVE (5) success factors for KAIZEN:

1. Teamwork, where staff works as a team towards achieving the desired improvement goal
2. Staff discipline contributes to Kaizen success
3. Staff morale from good working conditions, promotions, and other benefits give staff a sense of belonging and motivation
4. Quality Group, where staff can share knowledge, ideas, and skills
5. Staff suggestions for improvement, where all suggestions are welcomed, appreciated and considered

You can leverage other popular process improvements, such as PDCA to perform KAIZEN process improvements.

PDCA / PDSA

- PDCA / PDSA is a popular approach for doing Kaizen improvements.
- PDCA (Plan, Do, Check and Act) or PDSA (Plan, Do, Study, and Act) is an iterative four-step method used for continuous process improvement.
- Plan is establish the objectives and processes necessary to deliver results in accordance with the set goals.
- Do is to implement the plan and collect data for charting and analysis.
- Check / Study is checking and/or studying the actual results (measured and collected in "DO") and compare against the expected results (goals from the "PLAN") to determine any differences.
- ACT is to recommend actions on differences between actual and planned results. Further analyze the differences to determine their root causes and determine where to apply changes that will improve the performance of the process under investigation

35 Process classification framework®

The APQC Process Classification Framework® (PCF) is the de-facto global standard for characterizing business processes, and it is used in large and small companies, public and private, on every continent. This open standard has been used by business process management and benchmarking practitioners for more than 30 years to collect and compare performance data to find improvement possibilities.

APQC established the Process Classification Framework® ("PCF") as an open standard. Through process management and benchmarking, the PCF aims to aid organizational improvement. The PCF has been embraced as a common language for their processes by over 400 corporate and government organizations throughout the world. The PCF can be used by an organization to offer context for performance data and a basic structure for internal process reporting. When a company engages in APQC's benchmarking and/or best practices study, it can also provide PCF-based results. The PCF can be utilized to benefit any sector or organization because of the breadth of content it covers.

This enables organizations to map and compare any process at a high level of granularity, regardless of industry or size, to gain insight into where time is spent, the impact of changes on customers, stakeholders, employees, and leaders, and how processes compare to similar ones in other organizations. The APQC Process Classification Framework® (PCF) is a taxonomy of business processes that allows companies to identify, understand, and compare their processes to those of competitors.

The PCF is made up of goals, classifications, and processes from a variety of sectors. The framework was designed to allow companies to exchange and assess their business processes across industries, but it may also be used as an internal management tool to discover, standardize, and define business processes. The PCF has 543 individual process descriptions arranged into 34 categories across 11 objectives.

IT IS SURMOUNTING DIFFICULTIES
THAT MAKES HEROES.

Louis Pasteuri

Process classification framework®

Vision & strategy
- **Business long-term vision** — Define the business long-term vision
- **Business strategy** — Develop business strategy
- **Strategic initiatives** — Execute and measure strategic initiatives
- **Business models** — Develop and maintain business models

Products & services
- **Product/service program** — Govern and manage product/service development program
- **New products / services ideas** — Generate and define new product/service ideas
- **Products & services** — Develop products and services

Market & sell products & services
- **Understand markets** — Understand markets & customers
- **Marketing strategy** — Develop marketing strategy
- **Marketing plans** — Develop & manage marketing plans
- **Sales strategy** — Develop sales strategy
- **Sales plans** — Develop and manage sales plans

Physical products
- **Supply chain resources** — Plan for and align supply chain resources
- **Procurement of materials** — Procure materials and services
- **Production, assembly & test** — Produce/Assemble/Test product
- **Logistics & warehousing** — Manage logistics and warehousing

Deliver service
- **Service delivery and governance** — Establish service delivery governance and strategies
- **Service delivery resources** — Manage service delivery resources
- **Service to customers** — Deliver service to customer

Manage customer services
- **Services** — Develop client service strategy
- **Service contracts** — Manage client service contacts
- **After sales service** — Service products after sales
- **Customer satisfaction** — Evaluate client service operations/satisfaction

Develop & manage HR
- HR policies/strategies
- Recruit staff
- Staff training development
- Manage staff relations
- Reward & retain staff
- Redeploy and retire staff
- Manage staff data & analytics
- Manage& deliver staff comms

Manage IT
- Manage IT business
- Develop & manage IT strategy
- Develop & manage IT risk
- Develop & manage services & solutions
- Deploy services & solutions
- Create & manage support services & solutions

Manage financial resources
- Management accountings
- Revenue accounting
- General accounting
- Fixed asset project accounting
- Process payroll
- Process accounts payable / expenses
- Treasury operations
- Internal controls
- Manage taxes
- Manage international funds
- Perform global trade services

Manage assets
- Plan & acquire assets
- Design & construct productive assets
- Maintain productive assets
- Decommission product assets

Risk & compliance
- Manage enterprise risk
- Manage compliance
- Manage remediation efforts
- Manage business resilience

Manage relationships
- Investor relationships
- Government & industry relationships
- Board of directors
- Legal & ethical issues
- Manage PR

Develop business capabilities
- Business processes
- Portfolio & project management
- Manage change
- Enterprise quality
- Knowledge management
- Measure & benchmark
- Environmental health & safety
- Develop & deliver analytics

36 Knowledge management

Knowledge management (KM) is a collection of strategies for developing, sharing, utilizing, and managing an organization's knowledge and information. It is a multidisciplinary approach to accomplishing organizational goals through the most effective use of knowledge. Knowledge management is crucial since it increases an organization's decision-making efficiency. To ensure that all employees have access to the company's entire expertise, the appropriate knowledge must be available to those who require it. Knowledge management is a technique that can help a business get a competitive advantage by giving it access to the data it needs to increase sales and profitability. Knowledge management allows employees to exchange ideas and opinions that may be useful to their coworkers. By improving the efficiency of an organization's decision-making ability, KM improves productivity.

Organizational objectives such as increased performance, competitive advantage, innovation, sharing of lessons learned, integration, and continuous development are often the focus of knowledge management activities.

These initiatives overlap with organizational learning, but are distinguished by a greater emphasis on knowledge management as a strategic asset and fostering knowledge exchange. KM is a facilitator of organizational learning.

The importance of knowledge management dimensions of strategy, process, and measurement in the company has been recognised by study. The most critical resources for successful knowledge creation, dissemination, and application are people and the cultural norms that influence their behaviours; cognitive, social, and organisational learning processes are essential to the success of a knowledge management strategy; and measurement, benchmarking, and incentives are essential to accelerate the learning process and drive cultural change.

ACTION MAY NOT ALWAYS BRING
HAPPINESS, BUT THERE IS NO
HAPPINESS WITHOUT ACTION.

William James

Knowledge management

Knowledge management

Knowledge management is a process
KM is the process of creating, sharing, using & managing the information of an organization

KM requires a multi-discipline organizational approach
KM is a multidisciplinary approach to achieve organizational goals by making the best use of knowledge

Without knowledge management

Institutional knowledge lost
Employees with institutional knowledge leave the company and take their knowledge with them

Customer support issues
Support team members can't find quick answers to questions leading to customer dissatisfaction

Disconnect with teams
Teams in the organization are not on the same page

Project management issues
PM's keep repeating mistakes as PM best practices & Lessons Learned not shared

Types of knowledge

Factual knowledge — Knowledge from facts

Distributed knowledge — Spread out among many people

Empirical knowledge — Knowledge gained from observation

Procedural knowledge — Standard operating procedures

Experience knowledge — Knowledge from experience

Expert knowledge — Deep knowledge about a topic

Encoded knowledge — Written or symbol knowledge

Tacit knowledge — How to do things out of intuition

Explicit knowledge — Manuals and user guides are examples

Situation knowledge — Knowledge from community / cultures

The four components of knowledge management

People
Executives to sponsor & develop the organizational KM strategy with stakeholders & SME's to guide KM execution

Process
An organization requires an effective KM process to acquire and share knowledge that is readily available to all its employees

Content
Any kind of documented or electronic held knowledge including best practices and tips from colleagues and Subject Matter Experts

Strategy
All KM programs require a clear, documented, business strategy with measurable value to the business goals

Key questions for knowledge management

Is KM working as expected?
Is the knowledge management strategy & software working? What needs to changed?

Is KM delivering value?
Is the knowledge management strategy & tools delivering value to the organization?

Is KM implementation on track?
How is it known if the KM implementation on track and how is it being measured?

Has KM increased efficiency?
Has employee efficiency & productivity been improved with the use of KM?

The challenges of knowledge management

Knowledge sharing
Not everyone wants to store and sharing data

Data relevancy
With existing info overload unnecessary data needs avoidance

Security concerns
It is important that data is shared to the right people

Data requires processing
Data from one group may need to be changed to be meaningful to others

Rewarding KM supporters
It is important to identify KM contributors (if possible)

Knowledge contribution
Measuring knowledge contribution is hard so focus on the shared purpose

People turnover
People leaving is inevitable & KM data can disappear

KM roles & responsibilities
Choosing the right person to be responsible for KM is a success factor

Updating shared data
Keeping shared data updated is hard

KM technology
KM technology & tools constantly changing can be a challenge

Knowledge management strategy

KM Strategy
A good KM strategy adds value to business goals & operations

KM value proposition
KM boosts the efficiency of staff decision-making with access to firm expertise

KM tools & techniques
There are numerous KM tools & techniques such as content repository tools, knowledge search, decision support and big data

KM metrics / ROI
What metrics are used to measure the effectiveness of KM and its ROI?

The knowledge management process

1. Create info — New info is created every day in company

2. Identify info — Identify info critical to strategy & operations

3. Collect info — To make shareable with others

4. Review info — Evaluate its relevancy & applicability

5. Share info — Share info via documentation, KM sharing tools

6. Access info — Provide info access via. search & alert mechanisms

7. Use info — Use info to solve issues faster & make better decisions

37 The growth mindset

Based on the agile manifesto, an agile mindset will help an organization and its teams to achieve better results through continuous collaboration and communication. Understanding an agile mindset is vital to any business that wants to succeed with a continuous flow of incremental value. An organization adopting an Agile Mindset can increase its ability to deliver superior products, services, and solutions. It shifts a team from a focus on individuals to a focus on agile teams. By applying an Agile Mindset in conjunction with relevant processes and tools, teams can adapt to change and deliver incremental value to their customers.

Leaders with a growth mindset are open to new ideas and different ways of doing things where they embrace new challenges to persevere and think outside the box to develop new solutions to business problems. Leaders with a fixed mindset have a fear of failure and uncertainty and their focus is reducing these factors with extensive planning and micromanagement.

An agile mindset is focused on engaging and collaborating with others with the understanding that there are many different perspectives, on contributing to the team by learning and innovating to generate new ideas and approaches and staying flexible and open to change and differences to deliver incremental value to stakeholders. An agile mindset is the set of attitudes supporting an agile working environment that includes respect, collaboration, improvement and learning cycles, pride in ownership, focus on delivering value, and the ability to adapt to change.

The agile mindset involves being open to change while being flexible enough to adapt to the ever-changing needs of our clients. The agile mindset is an adaptive way of thinking that results in the rapid development of high-performing products and services. By leveraging the agile mindset, teams can adapt to change, learn more about their customers, deliver incremental value, and recognize the opportunity.∂

YOU HAVE POWER OVER YOUR MIND -
NOT OUTSIDE EVENTS. REALIZE THIS,
AND YOU WILL FIND STRENGTH.

Marcus Aurelius

The growth mindset

Leadership styles

Autocratic leadership
A task-oriented "command and control" style. They set clear expectations & directions to staff, tell them what to do & when and how to do it. No consultation.

Delegative leadership
A people-oriented leadership style is delegative. The leader doesn't provide much direction; decisions are made by staff. Can be good for motivated, high skilled small teams

Democratic leadership
A mix of task-oriented and people-oriented leadership styles. The leader gives guidance & direction, asks for feedback from staff but they make the final decisions

Agile leadership
Agile leadership is about creating self-organization where agile teams collaborate, learn from each other, get feedback from users & focused on quality & continuous learning

Why companies go agile

Faster delivery
The primary reason firms want to speed up software delivery

Handling changing priorities
Have greater ability to manage changing priorities by being able to adapt quickly

More productivity
By ensuring building right products efficiently as possible

Improved alignment
With greater stakeholder involvement at all stages results in better alignment

Software quality
A better approach in agile as quality is fixed, & scope & sequence are variable

Agile leaders

Focus on action
Agile leaders are more around doing

Focus on success
Agile leaders focus on transformation success

Remove roadblocks
Focus on removing obstacles

Constant learning
Agile leaders are constantly learning

Focus on people
Agile leaders focus maximising talent

Strong comms skills
A passion for comms & listening skills

Strong focus on priorities
An agile leader knows what to focus on

Drive & inspire
Ability to drive & inspire staff

Tine for reflection
They use reflection to think and learn

Openness & honesty
Clear ethics of ethics and integrity

Planning as they go
Plan & strategize as they go not before

Make decisions quickly
With limited information, make decisions fast

Create learning environment
Agile leaders aim to increase learning & adjust thinking on that learning

Visible & transparent
Make things visible & transparent

Flexibility
Use a high degree of flexibility in how they structure, organize, & execute the work

Feedback
Know how to give, receive and encourage useful feedback from staff

Create conditions
To promote collaboration & ownership

Introduce new practices
Providing coaching & mentoring to help staff to become better communicators, better adapting their plans to unplanned changes

Sets out new roles
An agile leader sets out new roles that describes specific skills sets that many staff need to ensure a more efficient flow of work

Agile styles

An Agile Leader creates an environment with a shared vision to be successful & provides a way forward of continual improvement in quality & efficiency

Coaching
Agile leaders focus on coaching and helping others in their development as leaders

Focus on process & quality
Sets expectations on quality, metrics to improve things & introducing new practices

Organizational shared vision
Facilitates orientation around a shared vision (town halls, group lunches, 'break-outs', outside speakers

Organization challenges & barriers
They understand the challenges & barriers teams run into, and help their teams overcome these barriers

Agile mindset

Respect
Respect starts with team & goes to staff at all levels of organization & the product itself

Collaboration
Collaboration is key to solve complex issues & at organization level will reduce handoffs to deliver

Continuous improvement
No process or leadership style or way of working is written in stone. Always room for improvement

Learning to fail
Allowing staff to try new ideas & possibly fail, gives staff an opportunity to learn and improve

Pride in ownership
Pride in what is delivered increases the desire to deliver quality work

Focus on delivering value
An agile team focuses on delivering the greatest value to customer

Ability to adapt to change
If unplanned changes are need, the organization adapts with it

38 Leading a digital transformation

Organizations are seeking ways to enhance business processes, build a strategic approach to expanding their business, and figure out the best ways to get their employees to participate in innovation and creativity. Integrating technology into process workflows is a critical component of today's business world, as is demonstrating innovative thinking through strategic and high-impact technological applications. Business leaders can change the way their organization operates and produce outstanding results for their firm and their employees. However, not all leaders have the ability to recognise what is right in front of them, but those who do have a great chance of succeeding. They see the broad picture and realise that they can make a difference. Transformational Leaders are those who can change things for the better.

Few people can see work processes, strategies, products, and services through the eyes of transformational leaders. As a result, they encourage their employees to think outside the box, streamline inefficient procedures, and replace inefficient systems.

Business Transformation Leadership uses research and case studies to demonstrate how transformative leaders can not only create new business models and services from the ground up but also adjust existing ones to compete effectively in today's market. From figuring out what they need to do to make a difference to putting out a plan to carry out their transformation campaign, we've got you covered. The ability to see a situation from a fresh perspective is crucial to business transformation.

Business Transformation Leaders have the abilities and methods to guide their teams through an organizational transition while instilling a sense of motivation in their employees to strive for continuous improvement in their services and products. It's all about attaining success with everyone engaged when it comes to transformation leadership. Companies are looking for ways to do things that no one else is doing or has done before. That is how they can make a difference and bring about change.

OUT OF YOUR VULNERABILITIES
WILL COME YOUR STRENGTH.

Sigmund Freud

Leading a digital transformation

Why transformation is hard?

Too much focus on technology
Too often the focus is on technology, with little to no thought about the process itself. It is merely an automation project.

Lack of leveraging data & analytics
DT is hard as it is about how effective the organization is at leveraging data to digitalize their business model & its value

Not really a transformation
After DT project, the character of the business does not change, it still does what it's always done, just better than it did before

Lack of know what transformation means
There is a lack of knowing what DT means to an organization's customers, partners, channels and employees

Insufficient CEO leadership
One major obstacle highlighted by staff of digital transformation is insufficient CEO leadership behind the company's initiatives

Too focused on optimising ASIS processes
Too much focus on optimising ASIS processes & not enough focus on mapping business model to customer's value creation

What is digital transformation?

Process transformation
A focus to reinvent processes to lower costs, reducing cycle times, or increasing quality using new technology & data

Business model transformation
Firms are looking how to transform the basic building blocks their business model and how value is delivered in their sector

Domain transformation
Business's are recognising that industry limits are becoming blurred with new tech that are creating new types of competitors

Transformation
Agile organizations understand that true transformation (learning, flexibility, autonomy) is required for sustainable transformation

Top reasons for failure

- A lack of a business case for transformation
- A lack of capabilities to drive innovation
- A lack of sense of urgency for investments
- A lack of CEO / board sponsorship
- A lack of focus on projects with impact
- Existing IT systems can't support digital goals

Qualities needed for leading digital transformation

Have a clear purpose going forward
They have an attitude of asking why? Are we adding technology to remain competitive, create a more productive workforce

Looking for the next opportunity
Successful digital leaders think ahead, always searching for the next opportunity today, tomorrow and in the future

They fix things that are broken & not right
Digital leaders fix what's broken and for what is not right. & will drive team problem solving, decision making & collaboration

Digital leaders are risk takers and experimenters
Digital leaders are risk-takers & experimenters who foster an environment for experimentation & innovation. Any innovative company will tell you that out of failure comes success

Digital leaders strive for collaborative partnerships
A successful digital leader knows collaborations from all over your business is key to be successful, and isn't afraid of embracing these types collaborative innovative partnerships to go forward

What is business disruption?

Disruption is a process
Disruption is a process, not a product or service, that occurs from the fringe to mainstream

Low end/new market
Originate in low-end (less demanding customers) or new market footholds

Quality standards are key
New firms don't catch on with mainstream customers until quality catches up with their standards

Some disruptions fail
Success is not a need for disruptors and some business can be disruptive but fail anyway

Different models
New firm's business model differs significantly from incumbent business's business model

Possible challenges of digital transformation

Employee pushback
Any change makes staff alarmed but in the digital age not changing is riskier for the firm & them

A digital strategy
A firm must have a digital strategy with a vision, a set goals to reach it

DT requires the right people
Transformation brings with many technical challenges & a company needs digital skilled people

DT requires flexibility
DT needs a fluid structure as new technology, data & customer experience

Budget constraints
Develop a DT plan over several phases for several years. Don't risk company over budgetary issues

DT elements

- Customer perception and touch points
- Sales proposition
- Performance management
- Automation
- Visualising work
- Digitising business
- New digital products
- Digital globalization

39 Leadership qualities & activities

Leadership is defined as a blend of emotions, attitudes, and behaviours used to guide employees. Empathy, problem-solving, commitment to staff development, open-mindedness, trustworthiness, and a good attitude are all leadership attributes that can assist people to navigate conflicts and challenges in the workplace.

A good leader has a clear vision and goals that he or she communicates to the rest of the team. They have a clear idea of what their team will do and how they will do it to achieve their goal. Character, clarity of thinking, centeredness, inner serenity, self-confidence, non-judgmental attitude, and devotion to one's cause are all prerequisites for leadership. Successful leaders are truthful in both their words and their actions, and they feel that trust is the most vital component of a healthy working relationship. Effective leaders recognise that arrogance suffocates the ability to work together successfully.

One of the characteristics of a good leader is the ability to communicate. It is just as vital for leaders to listen well as it is for them to communicate well. A successful leader has a clear vision, integrity, honesty, humility, and a laser-like concentration on what is required to assist their employees in achieving their objectives.

A leader who is confident in his or her capacity to lead and has a clear understanding of what is required to achieve the organization's objectives. A good leader ensures employee engagement and builds their team's confidence. They see the broad picture and know where the business is headed and how to get there. A good leader does not hesitate to hire individuals who are potentially better than them and is devoted to ensuring that their values are in line with the company.

SCIENCE IS ORGANIZED
KNOWLEDGE.

Immanuel Kant

Leadership qualities & activities

Business acumen

Big picture thinking — Leader sees "Big Picture" & how their decisions with others achieve results

Financial acumen — Staff hold a good grasp of the drivers of growth & profitability

Operations knowledge — Smart leaders develop their knowledge across all areas of business operations

Market knowledge — Staff have good grasp of the buying criteria & the value of every customer

Stay current — Understand the domain operating in helps to know future skills needed

Leadership qualities

Integrity & honesty — Integrity is about being honest and showing a consistent adherence to strong principles

Decision making — A key leadership competency is ability to make good decisions via. a decision-making process

Emotional / social intelligence — Ability to understand emotional situations in & to operate effectively in a many social situations.

Judicious — Able to see others' perspectives through being open to & considering others' points of view.

Handling company's politics — A leader has to be good political player who can manage political behaviour & know the game

Fortitude — Able to take planned risks & courage to stand up for what you believe & do the right thing

Handling conflicts — Have interpersonal skill that helps colleagues to avoid or resolve interpersonal conflicts

Influencing skills — A key part of leadership is about influencing & being an expert in social influence skills

Driving results

Accountability — Accountability for outcomes of their actions and decisions

Results focus — Leaders focus on results to achieve goals, solve problems & innovative ideas

Good comms — Effective leaders both provide direction to teams and listen to what they have to say

Trust — Building and maintaining trust within a team is always be a key priority for performance goals

Inspiration — Great leaders don't just drive results, they inspire staff to deliver superior outcomes

Feedback — It is key for staff performance, they need positive feedback

People skills

Good leaders strive to enhance team relationships and collaboration

Effective leaders know that delegating tasks is a sign of a strong leader not a sign of weakness

Good leaders is know how to spot talent-who can their your vision & strategies forward

The more honest and open a leader is, the more people will respect them as a strong leader

People motivators

- Recognizing contribution
- Thanking employees
- Setting effective goals
- Celebrating success
- Providing challenging work
- Asking for input and feedback
- Providing mentoring
- Allowing employee self governance

Change skills

Clarity of communications — Leaders need to understand the change, its implications & communicate them clearly

Strategic thinker — Good leaders are visionaries and look towards creating future strategic change

Coaching — Leaders need coaching skills to deal with staff who are struggling with change & how they react

Methodology knowhow — Leaders should have the ability to take advantage of change & project management methodologies

Handle uncertainty — Leaders coach staff sensitively to help them handle the uncertainty of change that comes

Collaboration — Good leaders work across boundaries to bring staff together to collaborate for greater good

Trust building — The speed of change is often proportional to the level of trust people have in their leaders

Commitment to change — Successful leaders are committed to planned change & resilient and persistent for results

Self development

Relationships building — Good leaders need to learn the skills for building good relationships in the workplace

Critical thinking skills — Leaders need to learn critical thinking skills to make intelligent rational decisions analysis based

Focus on results — Good leaders develop the skill of focusing on what matters most and know what impact it has

Self awareness — Great leaders are aware of their full potential as well as the areas to further develop

Good leadership

Corporate culture — Good leadership develops culture & staff understands the business vision & goals

A sense of belonging — Staff feel that they have a key role to play in the organization and that decisions for promotions are based on honesty and integrity for people whose talents and experience best fit the positions

Good leadership results — Good leadership results in good staff retention and morale & long-term business success

A DISCIPLINED MIND
BRINGS HAPPINESS.

Gautama Buddha

40 Transformation PMO leadership

Business transformation is a visible change, for customer experience, that modifies how end-users interact with the company and how the company offers products and services to end-user. Business Transformation is a strategy of change management. It aligns process, people and technology to organization strategy. It drives innovation and supports new business strategies. With customer experience, a company's main objective is to create positive experiences for the customers. "The End-to-End Transformation Journey". Business transformation is an integral part of the change management process. Without a proper change management process, business transformation projects end up achieving only a limited portion of their goals.

A transformation PMO can facilitate and communicate the shared vision for the business transformation project among stakeholders and target groups to foster support throughout the organization for needed changes.

A The importance of the PMO in an organization is crucial, but the role and responsibilities of the PMO are often misunderstood. A well-defined, properly managed PMO can provide a significant competitive advantage, improve business outcomes and accelerate enterprise performance and It can empower leaders to leverage key change initiatives by focusing on strategic planning and execution.

A transformation PMO can help disorganized change management processes that make it difficult to achieve transformation success. A consistent and effective business transformation program is difficult to establish and this is where a transformation PMO can play a key role. This one-page overview will give you the best practices to help you successfully manage business transformation initiatives. A successful transformation PMO knows that there is not one approach to managing a transformation project. It will require different approaches, tools, methods and techniques depending on your current environment and desired end state.

YOU MUST LOOK INTO PEOPLE,
AS WELL AS AT THEM.

Lord Chesterfield

Key questions for leadership

Vision
What is my vision and the direction that I want to take the organisation?

Alignment
How can I align the organization with your vision and mission?

Communication
How best to best communicate our goals and vision to the organisation?

Decisions
What key decisions do I need to make in the short term and long term?

Self improvement
What can I do to become a better leader? What is success to me?

Firm SWOT
What are the organisation's strengths, weaknesses and opportunities?

My value-add
What can I do to help the organisation be more successful?

Motivation
How can I keep my employees motivated during these challenging times?

Ongoing success
What I going well and not going well for the organisation?

Key questions for leadership

Competition
What is the competition doing in our marketplace?

Current goals
What are my current goals? How will I reach my goals?

Best focus area
If there was one focus area to improve, what would it be?

Barriers to success
What barriers to greater success have we as an organization?

Innovation
How can I create an organisation of collaboration and innovation?

Collaboration
How can I break down organisational silos so we can work together better

Transformation
How best to transform the business?

Customers
Do I understand the needs of our customers and stakeholders?

Operations
How can I achieve operational excellence?

Staff performance
How to improve employee performance and productivity?

Success factors for leadership

Self awareness

Leadership who can communicate the transformation change journey and its benefits A successful leader is self-aware and prioritize their personal development.

Lead by example

Good leaders are ethical, have integrity, leader by example, and have the ability to show respect, empathy, and encourage others to follow them.

Influencer

An influencer who can inspire, motivate and get the best out of their people.

Focus

A good leader has focus, a clear vision, is courageous, has integrity, honesty, humility, and a clear focus and direction.

Strategic planner

A strategic planner who believes in teamwork and collaboration.

Communications

A good communicator who has a clarity of purpose and is great at articulating their vision for an organisation.

Consensus

An accomplished leader leads by positive direction and builds agreement among an organisation.

Team success

A true leader focuses on helping his team succeed and their success is built upon the success of their team.

Focus on goals

An effective leader ensures that employees stay focused on the goals by keeping them motivated and helping them to achieve their goals

Success factors for leadership

Self awareness
Leadership who can communicate the transformation change journey and its benefits A successful leader is self-aware and prioritize their personal development.

Lead by example
Good leaders are ethical, have integrity, leader by example, and have the ability to show respect, empathy, and encourage others to follow them.

Influencer
An influencer who can inspire, motivate and get the best out of their people.

Focus
A good leader has focus, a clear vision, is courageous, has integrity, honesty, humility, and a clear focus and direction.

Strategic planner
A strategic planner who believes in teamwork and collaboration.

Communications
A good communicator who has a clarity of purpose and is great at articulating their vision for an organisation.

Consensus
An accomplished leader leads by positive direction and builds agreement among an organisation.

Team success
A true leader focuses on helping his team succeed and their success is built upon the success of their team.

Success factors for leadership

Team development
A good leader knows the strengths and weaknesses of their team members and focuses on developing them to reach their full potential.

Social skills
Communications, active listening and social skills are all key success factors.

Clear messages
Successful leaders can communicate clear messages and make complex ideas easy to understand for all employees and stakeholders.

Empowerment
Effective leaders now empower their employees, encourage strategic thinking, innovation, and be action-orientated.

Value of people
Good leaders recognise the value of people and surrounds themselves with great people who can work as a team to achieve shared goals.

PM skills
A successful leader nowadays requires good project management skills, leadership, and business strategy acumen.

Focus on goals
An effective leader ensures that employees stay focused on the goals by keeping them motivated and helping them to achieve their goals

The desired state for leadership

Vision
Everyone understands the vision and goals of the organization, and everyone has input into how they can be improved.

Results
There are improved results in customer satisfaction, sales, revenue, and employee productivity.

Strategic alignment
Improved strategic alignment from increased employee productivity, optimised processes and measured achievable results.

Agile proactive firm
An agile, proactive organisation that can react and change quickly and positively to changing customer and market needs

High morale
There is high morale, and the retention of employees is hight and employees want to stay with the company for long term success even when facing great challenges. .

Transparent comms
Communication is daily and transparent. Employees feel that they are an important part of the organisation.

Staff engagement
Employees have increased engagement and passion, which lead to higher levels of customer loyalty, service, innovation, and ultimately profits.

Talent development
The organisation has developed the best of its talent. for the benefit of the organisation.

Agile mindset
The organisation has agility, leadership has an agility mindset and employee are flexible and energised by the changes.

Business silos
Business silos broken down and employees across the enterprise are working and collaborating for shared success.

LIVE TRULY AND FORGIVE QUICKLY.

Paulo Coelho

Transformation PMO leadership

PMO leadership

Struggle with identity
Without focused PMO leadership, a PMO will struggle with its identity and the role it plays in its organization & a cause for future failure

Faces questionable value
A PMO which lacks strong PM focused leadership can have its growth stunted & its contributed organisation value questioned

PMO leadership enables a more strategic PMO role
A PMO leader with a good understanding of a firm's vision, strategy and processes will enable the PMO to become more strategic by knowing exactly how projects and programs map to strategic goals & helps to rally the PMO team behind their role

PMO leadership activities

PMO organization
Providing organizational leadership to develop & organise the PMO

PMO charter
Developing the PMO Charter to support organisation's goals

Project governance
Establishing governance, best practices & success criteria

Culture of value and improvement
Creating a culture of goal setting, value add, flexibility and continuous improvement

Project manager development
Develop leadership and project management skills of PM's

Change and transformation
Be a PMO transformational leader who promotes change & innovation

PMO maturity

Strategy
A PMO needs to have a strong commitment to their business goals (PMO value, alignment with firm goals & priorities, success criteria for project success & a plan for continuous improvement)

Operations
The PMO needs a clear PM process to establish consistency in project delivery supported by tools to promote knowledge transfer. Have a well defined comms plan & governance model for compliance

People
Build the right PMO team (right people, right job). Build long-term stakeholder relationships aligned with their business needs. Build a PMO team on the foundation of transparency

Metrics
Establish success criteria for PMO and projects. Have quality measures for improvement processes & defined performance metrics. Measure Customer Satisfaction (quality measure & success criteria)

PM & PMO leadership

Project management leadership
Project Management leadership focuses on the successful implementation of a project within scope, budget, and time constraints, assuming quality and customer satisfaction.

PMO leadership
A PMO leader has a multi-dimensional organisational role and responsibility that encompasses organisation building and the foundational elements necessary for running a business function

PMO leadership skills

| Manager skills | Direct others | Support people, schedules, tasks | Plan work & schedules | Monitor / supervise | Coordinate activities | Communicate effectively | Manage change |
| Leader skills | Inspire & guide with a vision | Motivate people | Enable change and empower people via coaching | Create & seek opportunities | Manage when needed | Obtain exec buy-in | |

The balance of PMO skills

Soft skills
- Relationship building
- Negotiation, Persuasion, Influence

Hard skills
- Analytical Thinking
- Social & Emotional Intelligence

General management skills
- Lead (Inspire, Transform)
- Direct (Vision, Mission, Values)
- Control (Monitor, Evaluate)
- Manage (Hire, Retain, Fire)

Portfolio management skills
- PM Methodology
- Estimating & Budgeting
- Portfolio Mgt. Processes
- Develop project metrics

Customer satisfaction
- Managing Expectations
- Develop Strategy & Alignment

Leverage skills
- Relationship Building
- Strategy Execution

41 Transformation leadership

Companies are expanding at a rapid rate by rethinking their sales, marketing, and service strategies, as well as changing the dynamics of how their employees interact with customers online. Digital transformation holds the promise of significant change. It means that an existing business process or service can be transformed into something different, even if it is still recognizable as the same business process or service. Often organizations think first about merging two formerly distinct processes or transforming one process into another. Although this might be ultimately necessary for some organizations, it often is not enough to transform an organization.

Whether you're an enterprise with 10,000 employees or a small company with 15 employees, the net-centric transformation will play a pivotal role in developing ways to work smarter and more productively. Digital technologies are changing the way companies do business; they are turning monolithic business models into nimble, interconnected businesses that work together in agile ways. This is called digital transformation.

Digital transformation means reimagining the way we live and work in a world by and with technology. Through this ongoing evolution of business processes, technology helps us to achieve inspiration through people's passions, innovation with cutting-edge solutions, and inclusion with our vast portfolio of products. It is the process of using emerging technologies that allow you to reimagine your business by focusing on new ways to engage with customers, support new business models or improve existing processes. It's about technology, data, process, and organizational change and meeting customers in the digital channels they already frequent. Digital transformation lets companies leverage data to better understand their customers and the marketplace as a whole and to free their data and share intelligence across their entire business.

THE ROOTS OF EDUCATION ARE BITTER, BUT THE FRUIT IS SWEET.

Aristotle

Transformation leadership

Transformation is difficult

Too much focus on technology
Too often the focus is on technology, with little to no thought about the process itself

A lack of effectiveness leveraging data
DT is hard as it is about how effective the organization is at leveraging data to digitalize their business model & its value

Not really a transformation
After the DT project, the character of the business does not change, it still does business as usual

A lack of knowing what transformation is...
There is a lack of knowing what DT means to an Organization's customers, partners, channels and employees

Insufficient CEO leadership
An issue often highlighted by staff of digital transformation is insufficient CEO leadership

Too much focus on 'ASIS" processes
Too much focus on optimising ASIS processes & not enough focus on mapping business model to customer's value creation

Digital transformation

Process transformation
A big focus to reinvent processes with the goal of lowering costs, reducing cycle times, or using new tech

Business model transformation
Business's are looking to see how to transform the basic building blocks their business model and how value is delivered in their sector

Domain transformation
Business's are recognising that industry limits are becoming blurred with new tech that are creating new types of competitors

Organization transformation
Agile Organizations understand that true transformation (learning, flexibility, autonomy) is required for sustainable transformation

Reasons for failure

- No business case for transformation
- no capabilities to drive innovation
- no sense of urgency to make investments
- A lack of CEO/ board sponsorship
- No focus on projects that impact business
- Existing IT systems can't support transformation

Qualities needed to lead a digital transformation

Have a clear purpose going forward
They have an attitude of asking why? Are we adding technology to remain competitive, create a more productive workforce

Digital leaders are risk takers and experimenters
Digital leaders are risk-takers & experimenters who foster a culture for experimentation & innovation, out of failure comes success

Always looking for the next opportunity
Successful digital leaders think ahead, always searching for the next opportunity today, tomorrow and in the future

Digital leaders strive for collaborative partnerships
A digital leader knows collaborations across the enterprise is key to be successful & isn't afraid of embracing collaborative partnerships

Fixing things that are broken and not right
Digital leaders fix what's broken and for what is not right. & will drive team problem solving, decision making & collaboration

What is business disruption?

Disruption = process
Disruption is a process, not a product or service, that occurs from the fringe to mainstream

Originates new markets
Originate in low-end (less demanding customers) or new market footholds

Quality standards
New firms don't catch on with primary customers until quality catches up with their standards

Some disrupters fail
Success is not a requirement for disruptors and some business can be disruptive but fail anyway

Different business model
New firm's business model differs significantly from incumbent business's business model

The challenges of digital transformation

Employee pushback
Changes makes staff alarmed but in the digital age not changing is riskier

A digital strategy
A firm must have a digital strategy with a vision, set goals & direction for it

Requires the right people
DT brings with it many technical challenges & a needs digital skilled people

Requires flexibility
DT needs a fluid company structure for new tech, data & customer focus

Manage budget
Have a plan over several phases. Don't risk firm over budgetary issues

Transformation elements

Customer perception & touch points	Sales proposition	Performance management	Automation	Visualizing work	Digitising the business	New digital products	Digital Globalization

42 Leading a Transformation Project

Organizations are seeking ways to enhance business processes, build a strategic approach to expanding their business, and figure out the best ways to get their employees to participate in innovation and creativity. Integrating technology into process workflows is a critical component of today's business world, as is demonstrating innovative thinking through strategic and high-impact technological applications.

Business leaders can change the way their organization operates and produce outstanding results for their firm and their employees. However, not all leaders have the ability to recognise what is right in front of them, but those who do have a great chance of succeeding. They see the broad picture and realise that they can make a difference. Transformational Leaders are those who can change things for the better.

Few people can see work processes, strategies, products, and services through the eyes of transformational leaders. As a result, they encourage their employees to think outside the box, streamline inefficient procedures, and replace inefficient systems.

Business Transformation Leadership uses research and case studies to demonstrate how transformative leaders can not only create new business models and services from the ground up but also adjust existing ones to compete effectively in today's market. From figuring out what they need to do to make a difference to putting out a plan to carry out their transformation campaign, we've got you covered.

The ability to see a situation from a fresh perspective is crucial to business transformation. Business Transformation Leaders have the abilities and methods to guide their teams through an organizational transition while instilling a sense of motivation in their employees to strive for continuous improvement in their services and products. It's all about attaining success with everyone engaged when it comes to transformation leadership.

Companies are looking for ways to do things that no one else is doing or has done before. That is how they can make a difference and bring about change. The world is waiting for transformational leadership to propel it ahead, whether that means shaking up stagnant enterprises to make them more competitive or rethinking historic systems in new and stimulating ways.

OPINION IS THE MEDIUM BETWEEN

KNOWLEDGE AND IGNORANCE.

Plato

Leading a transformation project

Organization design

Develop project charter
Establish Project Charter. Conduct summary ASIS analysis. Design alternative TOBE organization models. Educate leaders & assign design team

Assessment
Analyse processes &structure. Review culture. Benchmark similar organizations. Report to steering team

Design
Establish design guidelines & principles. Define business model. Redesign processes & structure. Verify the design

Transition
- Assign execution team
- Create detailed execution plans
- Train people in new roles
- Reconfigure systems / location

Implement
- Implement new org. models
- Monitor progress

Evaluate
- Assess performance vs. scorecard
- Make adjustments to design

Change management

Develop strategy
Review external environment. Assess ASIS strategy and goals. Set TOBE vision, strategy. Create project scorecard

Define the change & establish change network
Define what needs to change and why, then align to the strategy & goals

Determine the impacts
Determine change impacts, who & how impacted

Communication strategy
Develop a comms strategy to communicate & monitor feedback

Communication & training for desired skills
Communicate the change & provide training to business results

Best support for transition
Decide where support is required for a smooth transition

Measure change management process
Assess if the CM process was successful to achieve the goals

Business process reengineering

Define the business processes
Map the ASIS state (activities, workflows, rules, roles, relationships, technology)

Analyse business processes
Identify gaps & causes for improving organizational effectiveness, efficiency & strategic goal alignment

Identify process improvement opportunities
Identify & validate opportunities to act on the analysis results including transformation opportunities

Design TOBE processes
Use the improvements (time and cost based) with most impact on firm, efficiency aligned to strategic aims

Operationalize TOBE processes
Ensure new (TOBE) processes are embedded, communicated users trained on the new processes before implementation

Implement changes
Link TOBE implementation to other work streams: Org. Design, change management, enterprise performance management & agile PMO

Enterprise performance management

Strategy development & transition
Strategy Development determines an organization direction for strategy: mission, vision, strategic goals, Strategy Translation translates the strategy into particular organization actions with KPIs.

Business planning
Business Planning & Forecasting is a set of business activities planned against the strategy with forecasted results in a specific time period

Financial management
Financial Management refers to the set business processes done to close the financial records of a firm at the end of a period timely and accurate

Supply chain effectiveness
Supply Chain Effectiveness is the capabilities to manage an enterprise supply chain but also provide transparency to all parts of the value chain

Agile project management

Agile project management
Initiate, plan and execute agile process groups, especially those that can be employed in multiple domains, e.g. scrum

Agile program management
Provide a centralized view of status & metrics for all projects & for program as a whole. Resource mgmt. & load-balancing across projects

Agile portfolio management
Optimize ROI by analyzing proposed and current projects & programs. Value "responding to change over following a plan"

Project standards and quality
Ensure PM standards & quality across the org as high project maturity, a critical success factor for project success

Project efficiency & effectiveness
Agile PMO can improve efficiency and effectiveness by promoting the same PM standards and processes

Continuous improvement
The continuous improvement of agile PM is a critical success factor for an org undergoing transformation

43 Project Management Leadership

Leadership skills in project management are the basis for efficient communication, planning, execution, and control of large-scale projects. A Project Manager's ability to lead is critical to his or her success.

Knowing how to break down an issue into clearly stated objectives, break down large projects into manageable plans, and focus your team on the ultimate goals are all part of project management leadership skills.

To ensure the success of their initiatives, project managers must constantly improve their abilities. They must have a thorough understanding of the entire project life cycle, from planning to monitoring and controlling, including project scope, planning, scheduling, budgeting, change management, quality control, personnel, and communication.

The art of project management is completing a project on time and within budget. Project managers ensure that all tasks are done on time and within budget constraints. Projects must follow several processes to be successful, and a skilled project manager understands how to navigate these processes while preserving quality and client satisfaction.

Communicating with the project team, managing risks, and creating connections with stakeholders are just a few of the most critical aspects of being a project manager leader. A crucial requirement of a successful project management leader is that all stakeholders are on board for business success as well as personal career success.

A great Project Manager is more than a manager; he is a leader who can communicate and motivate others to reach the project's end goal. The leadership of a project manager is focused on completing a project within the scope, budget, and schedule restrictions while ensuring quality and customer satisfaction.

NEVER INTERRUPT YOUR ENEMY
WHEN HE IS MAKING A MISTAKE.

Napoleon Bonaparte

Project management leadership

Project manager skills

Leadership	Negotiation	Scheduling	Budgeting	Risk management
A PM leads a team as well as manage them, to be able to inspire others & lead effectively	PM's require good negotiation skills to resolve team & stakeholders issues by finding win-win options	A PM needs the core project management skill of being able schedule to demonstrate competence	Budget management is a key leadership skill to keep clear oversight of cost control for a project	A PM who is given complex, transformative, projects knows effective risk management is key
Communications	**Sharing a vision**	**Competence**	**Problem solving**	**Delegator**
Excellent comms skills are essential for PM to communicate effectively with people at all levels of a firm	Seeing the 'bigger picture' & communicating to others is a key factor for being a successful project manager	For a leader to gain the respect and trust of their team, a PM needs to demonstrate that they are competent and capable	A good PM has excellent problem solving skills & be resourceful and creative in their general approach to solving problems that arise	A successful PM must be able to delegate effectively by assigning tasks to the right people for the best possible results
Positive attitude	**Integrity**	**Coolness**	**Team builder**	**Decision making**
A PM with a positive attitude makes it a pleasure to engage with & their enthusiasm influences others to be positive too	A key skill for a PM is the ability to gain the trust of their project team by demonstrating the adherence to values and honesty	It is a big probability that will all plans, unexpected problems occur & a good PM will never panic and keep cool when things go wrong	A PM knows that a happy, competent, confident team with a common purpose is key for a successful project outcome	A PM must have the ability & confidence to make decisions which will have a direct impact of a successful project outcome
Contract management	**Coaching**	**Meetings management**	**Quality management**	**Project recovery**
Part of managing projects often involves managing suppliers from IT suppliers and service providers	A successful PM will be able to coach employees who don't much project experience for top performance	Being able to manage meetings is a critical skill for a PM to make sure time is well spent & productive	An overlooked PM skill is quality management that ensures a product that is delivered is fit for purpose	Not all projects go to plan and a key PM skill is the ability to turn around a poorly performing team and project

PM training

PM software too training	PM basics	Advanced PM skills	Leadership training	Business training	PMP preparation	PM certificate / degree	Agile project management

Possible PM career path

Project team member	Associate PM	Project manager	Senior project manager	Program manager	PMO manager	PMO director	Chief projects officer

Hard skills

Multilingual	Industry experience	Work breakdown	PMP certification	MS project	Risk management
MS office	Project charter prep,	Scheduling	Project management degree	PM software tools	Budget management

Soft skills

Integrity	Dependability	Communications	Open mindedness	Problem solving	Creativity
Team work	Critical thinking	Adaptability	Organization	Willingness to learn	Empathy

44 Global Project Management

More firms are undertaking worldwide projects as a result of increased globalisation, yet virtual project teams frequently fail to achieve appropriate levels of efficiency and quality for global projects. The mere fact that the initiatives are to be carried out virtually poses a significant challenge.

Global project management necessitates the development of effective project management systems that are adaptable enough to deal with the unique issues that virtual teams face in complicated situations. A global project's alignment of the primary project procedures, as well as the cultural and environmental aspects that influence the project, is a critical success factor.

Virtual work face-to-face is difficult; technology has a role; processes must be adapted to match individual circumstances; informal socialisation is imp, and; and how projects are defined can have a major impact. Organizations can benefit from new advancements in communication and technology to better execute worldwide initiatives.

Project managers will learn how to form and manage virtual teams with practical advice on communication, cultural challenges, and effective virtual team management in Global Project Management Best Practices. It also contains approaches for managing projects and teams in low- and high-context cultures.

These best practices describe how effective project managers have established and managed worldwide projects. It discusses leadership, cultural diversity, and communications to these multi-country, multi-firm partnerships, as well as crucial success aspects including overcoming cultural gaps and managing virtual teams.

PRIDE COSTS US MORE THAN HUNGER, THIRST, AND COLD.

Thomas Jefferson

Global project management

Global PM benefits

Access to new skills and perspectives
Access to local knowledge, skills, experience and new perspectives

Lower operational costs
Global working allows lower taxes & lower employee wages

Challenges with global projects

Global team communication is difficult
Even with technology, global team communications is difficult (different companies, expectations, ethics, languages, times, locations & cultures)

More work done
Global working 24-hour coverage as other countries sleep

Time differences can be awkward
Organising calls can be a challenge **9 am** GMT is **4 am** New York is **1.30 pm** Mumbai India is **6 pm** Sydney

Different worksyles & cultures
Cultural variations in workstyles & expectations and miscommunications often leads to difficulties

Global PM cultural preparation

Time can mean different things
Time is a flexible concept in some cultures where meetings rarely start on time & deadlines & milestones are just a guide to work to

Adject leadership approach to culture
Some cultures are comfortable with a collaborative style or working where other cultures, formality is more acceptable

Understand local management hierarchies
Staff working in different cultures or companies with strong hierarchical structures may not take direction from a Global PM

Saving face is a big issue in some cultures
Some cultures find it easy to admit a mistake but in other cultures losing face is a complex issue that cannot be underestimated

Set expectations with stakeholders
It is key to manage upwards and ensure that senior stakeholders understand the constraints of a global project

Find the right tools for a global project
Define a tool strategy for communications, collaborative working, project tracking & reporting & tools for project

Global PM role

Clarify scope & objectives
Clarify scope & objectives & enlist team support

Review definition of deliverables
Review & agree the definition of deliverables

Review project plan
Review plan for people, resources & budget

Change management
Manage changes and assess their impacts

Manage performance
Manage performance by tracking progress

Manage risks/
Review risks/ mitigation actions

Manage comms
Ensure good communications

Manage quality
Is work quality being checked

Goals and deadlines
Manage goals, targets & deadlines

Manage team
Assess team morale

Build trust in project team
Listening to team members shows you care. Provide mentorship where needed. Take accountability for actions and mistakes. Embrace failure and create positive actions. Be honest & consistent with what you say. Encourage collaboration & show respect for all

Handle conflict in the project team
Global collaboration on project , despite its incredible benefits to an organization, unfortunately, also leads to conflicts. Acknowledge there is a conflict and take appropriate measures to resolve it. Ensure team knows project success is the priority, listen to all views and make informed decisions

Respect for different cultures

Know different holidays
Be sensitive countries have different Government holidays

Appreciate work/life balance
Understand that there is a life outside work for members

Encourage full participation
Ensure all members participate in meetings

Cultural words

Respect | Patience | Listening | Silence | Observation | Openness | Divergence

Use of English language

Use common words
Restrict English words to their most formal common use with few meanings

Alternative spellings
Become aware of alternate spellings (e.g. organization)

Basic grammar rules
Conform to basic grammar rules more strictly

Avoid sports or literature terms
Avoid terms from sports ("can't get to first base") or literature ("Catch-22")

45 Leadership Qualities

Leadership is defined as a blend of emotions, attitudes, and behaviours used to guide employees. Empathy, problem-solving, commitment to staff development, open-mindedness, trustworthiness, and a good attitude are all leadership attributes that can assist people to navigate conflicts and challenges in the workplace.

A good leader has a clear vision and goals that he or she communicates to the rest of the team. They have a clear idea of what their team will do and how they will do it to achieve their goal. Character, clarity of thinking, centeredness, inner serenity, self--confidence, non-judgmental attitude, and devotion to one's cause are all prerequisites for leadership. Successful leaders are truthful in both their words and their actions, and they feel that trust is the most vital component of a healthy working relationship. Effective leaders recognise that arrogance suffocates the ability to work together successfully.

One of the characteristics of a good leader is the ability to communicate. It is just as vital for leaders to listen well as it is for them to communicate well. A successful leader has a clear vision, integrity, honesty, humility, and a laser-like concentration on what is required to assist their employees in achieving their objectives.

A leader who is confident in his or her capacity to lead and has a clear understanding of what is required to achieve the organization's objectives.

A good leader ensures employee engagement and builds their team's confidence. They see the broad picture and know where the business is headed and how to get there. A good leader does not hesitate to hire individuals who are potentially better than them and is devoted to ensuring that their values are in line with the company.

MAY YOU ALWAYS
KEEP YOUR YOUTH.

Mark Twain

Leadership qualities

Category	Big picture thinking	Financial acumen	Operations knowledge	Market knowledge	Future Skills
Business acumen	Sees "Big Picture" & how to achieve results	Staff hold a good knowhow of the drivers of growth	Leaders develop their know how across all operations	Staff have good grasp of the value of every customer	Understand the future skills needed to succeed
Leadership qualities	**Integrity & honesty** — Integrity is about honesty and showing a strong adherence to ethical principles // **Decision making** — The leadership ability to make good decisions via. a decision-making process	**Emotional / social intelligence** — Ability to understand emotional situations & to operate effectively in a many social situations // **Judicious** — Able to see others' perspectives through being open to & considering others' points of view	**Handling company politics** — A leader has to be good political player who can manage political behaviour & know the game // **Fortitude** — Able to take planned risks & courage to stand up for what you believe & do the right thing	**Handling conflicts** — Have interpersonal skill that helps colleagues to avoid or resolve interpersonal conflicts	**Influencing skills** — A key part of leadership is about influencing & being an expert in social influence skills
Results driven		**Accountability** — Accountability is by taking responsibility for outcomes of their actions and decisions // **Results focus** — Leaders focus on results to achieve goals, solve problems & develop ideas	**Good comms** — Effective leaders both provide direction to their teams and listen to what they have to say // **Trust** — Building and maintaining trust within a team is always be a key priority for performance goals	**Inspiration** — Great leaders don't just drive results, they inspire staff to deliver superior outcomes // **Feedback** — Constructive feedback is critical for development & performance measurement	
People skills		Good leaders constantly strive to effectively enhance team relationships and collaboration	Effective leaders know that delegating tasks is a sign of a strong leader not a sign of weakness	Good leaders is know how to spot talent-who can their your vision & strategies forward	The more honest and open a leader is, the more people will respect them as a strong leader
People motivators	Recognizing contribution // Thanking employees	Setting effective goals // Celebrating success	Providing challenging work // Asking for feedback and inputs	Providing mentoring // Employee self governance	
Change skills		**Clarity of communications** — Leaders need to understand the change, its implications and communicate them clearly // **Strategic thinker** — Good leaders are visionaries and look towards creating strategic future change plans	**Coaching** — Leaders need coaching skills to deal with staff who are struggling with change & how they react // **Methodology knowhow** — Leaders should have the ability to take advantage of change & project management methodologies	**Handle uncertainty** — Leaders coach staff sensitively to help them handle the uncertainty of change that comes // **Collaboration** — Good leaders work across boundaries to bring staff together to collaborate for greater good	**Trust building** — The speed of change is often proportional to the level of trust people have in their leaders // **Commitment to change** — Successful leaders are committed to planned change & resilient and persistent for results
Self development	**Relationship building** — Good leaders need to learn the skills for building good working relationships at work	**Critical thinking skills** — Leaders need to learn critical thinking skills to make intelligent rational decisions analysis based	**Focus on results** — Good leaders develop the skill of focusing on what matters most and know what impact it has	**Self awareness** — Great leaders are aware of their full potential as well as the areas to further develop	
Good leadership		**Corporate culture** — Good leadership develops culture & staff understands the business vision & goals	**A sense of belonging** — Staff feel that they have a key role to play in the organisation and that decisions for promotions are based on honesty and integrity for people whose talents and experience best fit the positions	**The results of good leadership** — Good leadership results in good staff retention and morale & long-term business success	

46 Leading Remote Workers

Leading remote teams effectively is an essential ability for today's leaders, but it's a new problem for the majority of managers. It necessitates new techniques and procedures that, when properly implemented, can offer extremely favourable results. Leading remote workers is a highly effective approach to keeping top talent while also increasing productivity and engagement. Leading a high-performing team may be difficult even in the best of conditions. The process of managing remote employees becomes considerably more difficult when team members work from home, are geographically dispersed, and have different cultural backgrounds.

Global enterprises are increasingly relying on globally distributed teams to offer high performance and innovation. Cultural differences, on the other hand, frequently result in drastically different perceptions, and it is up to team leaders to bridge those gaps. Body language, listening, clarification, and confirmation are all common comms issues for remote staff.

Your remote working workforce will not only be productive but thrive in this new environment if you understand the obstacles, have a clear plan for tackling remote work and have adequate management support.

The major problems that a leader will confront are social connections, communication, and isolation, but they can all be addressed with the appropriate plan. Remote professionals have a variety of problems, including how to interact successfully via phone, email, and instant messaging.

Working remotely might be tough for certain people, so as an employer, you should devise a strategy to support your employees. The difficulties of establishing appropriate communication when face-to-face contact is limited, as well as social isolation and a lack of understanding owing to poor listening by team members and project participants.

The leader should describe the team's objective and ensure that there is a clear direction for performing the tasks necessary to complete your mission by clarifying roles and expectations.

A WELL ADJUSTED PERSON IS ONE
WHO MAKES THE SAME MISTAKE
TWICE WITHOUT GETTING NERVOUS.

Alexander Hamilton

Leading remote workers

Remote working strategies

On the same page — All stakeholders align on expectations, tools & metrics

PMO tool strategy — A PMO needs a tools strategy for meetings, reporting, collaborating

Celebrate Success — Celebrate remote staff achievements on team calls

Time zone sensitivity — Status & governance meetings must consider different time zones

Remote meetings — Meeting need to be more frequent, short & effective with agenda and actions

Train remote workers — Train remote workers on how to work effectively (online training/ practices)

Remote expectations — A PMO must set expectations on PM reporting & governance

Plan for feedback — PMO and PM's need to have a comms plan that allows feedback

Exec Q&A sessions — Hold calls with execs for updates & reinforce company culture

Remote project management — A PM must set expectations, vision, timeline & goals for a remote project

Foster team spirit — Plan to foster team spirit by sharing knowledge, ideas & personal info

Use snail mail — Use post to send cards or recognition awards to increases sense of belonging

Remote needs — Remote PM's need to update tasks & status daily for transparency

Plan for PMO value — it is always a success factor for a PMO to show visible added value

Take the lead — Identify projects or task where remote staff can take the lead

Organizational questions

Network & data — What networks & firm data should be accessible remotely?

Staff time in office — How much time will be spent in the office, and when and if any at all?

Tech and support — What tech support and equipment is needed and who will provide it?

Workplace communications — How and what tech solution to maintain high level of workplace communication?

Meetings & projects — How meetings & projects will be managed & accountable?

Collaboration / productivity tools

Office 365 — Collaborate with online versions of Word, Excel, PowerPoint, and OneNote.

Chat & collaboration — Chat and collaboration tools (Trello, Slack, Meet & Chat)

Video calling — Video calling apps (Google Hangout Meet & Chat, Skype)

Screen sharing — Screen sharing tools (MS teams, Zoom, TeamViewer)

Cloud based tools software features

MS office — Integration with MS Office: Word, Excel, PPT

Communications — Able to capture all tasks, documents & project info

MS project integration — MS Project users who need the more complex features of this software

Use templates — Use templates to bring consistency & simplicity to key PM processes

Simple to use — Ease of use promotes use of a tool. A tool underused is a waste of money

Central document repository — Allows integration of documents, tasks, & key project info with dashboards

SharePoint integration — Able to leverage document mgt. & collaboration capabilities of SharePoint

Document management — Allows check-in. check out, version control with docs accessible anytime

Project status — Project status reports with project info updates in real time

Automated metrics — The ability to see automated generated metric reports

Benefits from remote working

Staff retention — Staff have flexibility they need with better work-life balance

Happier, healthier staff — Lack of commuting for staff gives them more time, money & less stress

Larger pool of talent — For young staff, workplace flexibility is key factor they consider for a new role.

Autonomous staff — Remote working lets staff work how it is best for them in time & location

Leverage technology — Tech, a key remote working enabler to foster teamwork & collaboration

Remote working best practices

Remote working offers flexibility, less cost & time wasted commuting with the ability to live anywhere. Increased productivity from less distractions

Have boundaries — Have boundaries for work & life

Work visibility — Plan to make yourself visible at work

Be available — Publicise your availability to speak

Online shared photo board — Have a shared online board for photos

Use chat tool — For ongoing talks with team members

Leading remote workers

Virtual team challenges

Misunderstandings	**Comms incompatibility**	**Different work ethics**	**Lack of clarity**	**Second guessing**
Issue from poor comms	Comms method preferences	Differences in work ways	Lack of clarity and direction	Frequent second-guessing
Lack of ownership	**Asking the right questions**	**Delegation difficulty**	**Lack of common understanding difficulties**	
Lack of remote owners	Not asking right questions	Difficulty with delegation	Comms difficulties without body language & tone-of-voice	

Virtual team leadership

Self motivated leader	**Excellent comms skills**	**Embrace VT technology**	**Show trust in team**	**Realistic expectations**
A VT leader needs to be able to lead a VT team without a lot of direction	Without the benefit of body language, a VT leader needs good clear comms skills	A leader needs to be able to use all types of virtual team technologies for comms	A VT leader must show trust to motivate VT members	A leader needs to have realistic expectations of VT team capabilities

Virtual team members

Good people	**Good comms skills**	**Emotional intelligence**	**Self starters**
Good virtual teams must start with good exceptional self starters	Virtual team members need to have good communication and listening skills	VT staff need a high degree of E.I. to know what they're feeling, what their emotions mean, &how these emotions can affect other people	VT staff need to be self-starters who work on own to achieve goals

Team success

Trust	**Collaboration**	**Motivation**	**Autonomous**	**Good communications**

Technology

Video conferencing	**Comms & chat tools**	**Digital boards**	**Email**	**Snail mail**
Use video conferencing for face-to-face meetings	Use comms tools for chat for quick comms within team	Use digital boards for team sharing / interactions	Use email to send complex info and not time-sensitive	Use normal post to send cards & awards

Guiding principles

Create team agreement	**Advance agenda**	**Start with a purpose**	**Avoid monologues**	**Use technology**
To run meetings including member back-up , if a member cannot make it.	Send agenda and meeting material 24 hours in advance with specific actions	Start with a purpose and why team participation is critical for success	Call people's name to stimulate collaboration and participation.	Use collaboration and video capabilities for virtual meetings
Improvement	**Stakeholder motivation**	**Finish on time**	**Clarify tasks & processes**	
Ask everyone (+) or (-) feedback at meeting end to improve effectiveness	Invite a key stakeholder for a brief hello & message to motivate the team	Go to 50 minutes rule so people can move from one meeting to another	Clarify meeting tasks & processes, not just goals & roles	

Before the meeting practices

Prepare key topics	**Assign a leader**	**Use an ice breaker**	**Meeting agreements**	**Clarify expectations**
Prepare key topics, meeting goals & desired outcomes	Assign a leader of the meeting & rotate them	Plan an ice breaker & greetings to start meeting	Review agreements to ensure equal participation	Clarify the expectations & roles of team member

During the meeting

Be emphatic about starting the meeting on time this will set the meeting tone	Listen attentively, greetings and check in with their status	State meeting aims & desired outcomes at meeting end	Start meeting reviewing status of past actions & achievements

After the meeting practices

Record actions	**Clarify resolutions**	**Plan next meeting**	**Document outcomes**
Record actions, owners, dates	Clarify resolutions & time	Plan next meeting agenda with the team	Document meeting outcomes
Follow-up 1:1	**Stay connected**	**Follow through**	**Team effectiveness**
Follow up on 1:1 with members	Stay focused on goals	Follow through all actions until completion	Measure team effectiveness

47 Chief Information Officer

A Chief Information Officer (CIO) is a high-ranking executive responsible for managing and successfully implementing the information and computer technology systems of a company. A CIO must be agile, responding quickly to trends, changes, and the needs of the organization, its people, and those it serves.

It is now quite common for CIOs to be appointed from the business side of an organization, especially if they have PM skills as they provide a critical interface between the business needs, user needs & technology used in the work.

CIOs are business-orientated because they provide a critical interface between the business needs, user needs & technology used in the work.

CIOs need knowledge in business and technology to manage IT resources and to manage and plan: technology including policy and practice development, planning, budgeting, resourcing and training.

CIOs play a key role in helping to control costs & increase profits via the use of technology, and to limit potential organisational damage by setting up appropriate IT controls for disaster recovery.

IT IS BETTER TO OFFER NO EXCUSE
THAN A BAD ONE.

George Washington

Chief information officer

Reasons for a CIO

Be a critical interface for business
CIOs play a key role in businesses as they provide a critical interface between the business needs, user needs & technology used in the work

Require knowledge of business and technology
CIOs need both knowledge in business and technology to manage IT resources and to manage and plan technology including policy, development, planning, budgeting, resourcing and training

Role in controlling costs & improving costs
CIOs play a key role in helping to control costs & increase profits via the use of technology, and to limit potential organisational damage by setting up appropriate IT controls for disaster recovery

The CIO role

CIO is a business leader
A CIO has a role of a business leader and is responsible for several business functions

IT objectives and strategies
Setting aims and strategies for the IT team to provide leadership & direction

CIO is a recruiter
CIO's also have the responsibility of recruiting & it is key that they work proactively to source and nurture the best employees possible

Selection & implementation of technologies
Selecting and implementing technology to streamline operations &d optimize strategic benefits

Digital services expectations
Customers are expecting digital services as part of their relationship with an organization, CIOs have more product-oriented responsibilities now

Leveraging technology to leverage CX
Designing and customizing technological systems and platforms to improve customer experience

CIO skills & qualities

Knowledge of the business
CIOs' knowledge of the business, leadership capabilities and strategic perspectives have taken precedence over technical skills

Demonstrate flexibility
CIO's have to be flexible to adapt not only to a changing workplace & also to a changing world

Diplomatic demeanour
Technology touches all parts of an organisation, and the CIO needs ability to make connections & decisions with a diplomatic approach

Crisis and change management
The CIO has to know how to effectively manage change & pushback with adoption of new tech.

Emerging technologies
CIO's are on top of emerging trends in business technology and the digital tools that will enable improved CX, revenue & profits

Employee empathy
By seeking to understand their employees, a CIO leadership style will be more effective

Techno speak translator
A CIO must be able to both understand the technical pros and cons of technologies and explain those to other decision makers

Board level leadership skills
CIOs must possess or acquire board-level leadership skills

CIO priorities & activities

New business models
Explore new business models with digital not just digitize "ASIS"

Embrace change
Embrace the pace of change

Change leadership
Improving change leadership and management

Digital
Increasing digital footprint in organisation

Customer engagement
Increase customer engagement via. improved customer experience

Digital in business strategy
Driving digital transformation in the company business strategy

Driving innovation
Driving innovation / increase relevance of IT within the firm

Cybersecurity
Increasing focus on privacy and security of customer data

Products
Get more involved in product development

Customer focus
Increasingly customer focus internally and externally

Transformation
Establishing thought leadership for driving digital transformation

Internal clients
Being more responsive to internal clients in firm

Find & invest in people
Invest more in staff skills & capabilities & finding and keep top IT talent

Automation
Process automation & supply chain digitization

Strategy alignment
Enabling organisation and strategy alignment

Improve revenue & profits
Move the revenue and profit needle

Technologies focus

Business intelligence	5G & mobile technology	CRM
Analytics (BI, AI, RPA)	SaaS, IaaS, Cloud computing	IT management
Legacy reduction	Virtualization	
Digital technologies	Cybersecurity	

CIO personal matrix

This simple tool lets a CIO map out where there planned actions will have have the biggest effect. It shows where are the quick wins and the longer-term strategic goals and where to stop stop making unnecessary efforts.

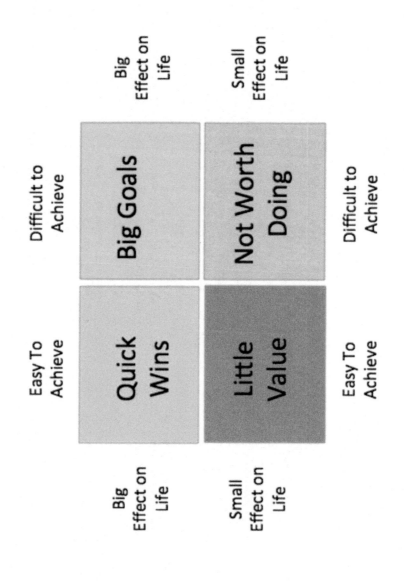

	Easy To Achieve	Difficult to Achieve
Big Effect on Life	Quick Wins	Big Goals
Small Effect on Life	Little Value	Not Worth Doing

Quick Wins = Big effect on Life and Easy to Achieve
Big Goals = Big Effect on Life and Difficult to Achieve

- This is a simple exercise for a CIO to brainstorm their potential actions and then you decide where they sit on this **Personal Impact Matrix.**

- Quick Wins represent **easy opportunities** to achieve which will motivate you towards your longer term big goals which are more difficult to achieve but offer greater reward.

- Finally it shows actions that you should consider to **stop doing** as they offer limited value to organization success.

- A key success factor in life is to know where to **focus and prioritise** your energy & actions for maximum value.

48 Chief Technology Officer

A Chief Technology Officer(CTO) is an executive who is responsible for the management of an organization's research and development (R&D) as well as its technological needs.

As a leader in an organization, a CTO must demonstrate their understanding of the business' needs when developing and implementing strategic plans. To support these plans, a CTO must know subject areas such as finance, business modelling, and project management.

A CTO is well-versed in technology having accumulated vast technical experience by having worked on different levels of development and have dealt with many challenges. They would know the different programming languages, their major uses with pros and cons. A CTO needs to be familiar with all relevant technology trends and technological infrastructures, and be ready to deploy them within his or her company. Extensive knowledge, a fine-grained sensitivity to the human aspects of all process deployments, and a deep understanding of business considerations are also essential.

A CTO may envision how technology will be used within the company while setting the technical strategy for the company. This CTO will also look at how to further implement new technologies within the company to ensure its success. As technology focuses more on integrating applications and processes, Big Data, moving data to the cloud, CTOs must keep abreast of streaming analytics, and cloud technology to remain innovative and stay competitive.

They develop policies and procedures and use technology to enhance products and services that focus on external customers. The CTO also develops strategies to increase revenue and performs a cost-benefit analysis and return-on-investment analysis.

WHAT WE ACHIEVE INWARDLY
WILL CHANGE OUTER REALITY.

Plutarch

Chief technology officer

CTO role

Developing the technology strategy
Developing the company's strategy for technology use

Ensuring best use of technology
Ensuring technologies are used efficiently, profitably & securely

Evaluation of new technology
Evaluating and implementing new systems and infrastructure

Increasing firm's revenue
Increasing the company's top line

The implementation & strategy glue
Be the glue for technology implementation & product strategy.

A CTO is the firm's top technology architect
The CTO is product & strategy "future" focused towards the bigger picture & not involved in day-to-day tech issues and activities

Implementing infrastructure
A CTO guides the business through the growing pains of implementing new technologies, securing data, and maintaining networks

Customer focus
A CTO focuses on the target markets of the business & deploys IT projects to support positive customer experiences

Thought leadership
A CTO plays a key role in developing the corporate strategy regarding the infrastructure and capital needed to achieve goals

Technology planning
A CTO determines which new technologies a business should apply to its current processes to drive continued success

Engineering teams
Managing the engineering & developer teams

Understanding all technologies
Understand all technologies in a company

Working with 3rd party vendors
Collaborating with vendors on tech solutions

Aligning enterprise architecture
Aligning EA with business priorities

Reviewing technologies for external services
Reviewing technology to improve the firm's external products and services for short & long term needs

CTO responsibilities

Overseeing IT departments
Overseeing IT operations & departments

Streamlining business processes
Using technology to streamline business processes

Increasing the firm's bottom line
Increasing firm's net income after expenses

Focus on staff and business units
Focusing on staff and business needs

Managing all the IT infrastructure
A CIO is focused on day-to-day operations, focus on mission critical systems, and overall security

CTO technical experience

- Big data engineering
- Network & cloud
- DevOps
- AI
- Project management
- UX design
- Strategic business mgt.
- Backend (web, database)
- IT & security mgt..
- Software architecture
- Internet of things (IOT)

CTO education & soft skills

Degree & MBA
A degree in a subject & MBA (opt.)

Communications
Every CTO needs to be able to communicate effectively to their respective audiences

Customer focused
Make sure every decision made is customer focused

Vision ability
A key functions as CTO is to set product and technical vision

Strategic thinking
CTOs need the ability to focus on the Big Picture to think strategically

People inspiration skills
A CTO needs to inspire others to get behind their vision so they can execute on the technology projects

Modern leadership
Deliver modern leadership around authenticity and empathy

Build an effective ecosystem
Able to build ecosystem of partners & platforms for innovation & deliver an technology strategy

- Communications
- Leadership
- Teamwork
- Problem solving
- Conflict management

Keep ego in check
Check your ego at the door with your staff

Understand business
Understand business needs and emerging technologies

CTO best practices

Technology sake
Don't build tech for technology's sake

Alternatives
Constantly look at tech alternatives

Stay in touch
Stay in touch with everything that's going on & emerging technology trends

49 Strategy Development

A strategy is a set of instructions for achieving a given goal. The strategy of an organization directs its course, establishes priorities, and keeps the organization on track and focused. A competitive strategy sets the stage for the development and marketing of specific programs, products, and services. The process of researching and discovering strategic possibilities, selecting the most promising, and deciding how resources will be deployed across the company to meet objectives is known as strategy development.

A competitive strategy's main goal is to gain a competitive edge, increase existing client loyalty, and outperform competitors. To get the most effective results, a smart strategy is founded on a few important points of the current situation. Effective marketing, operational, and financial plans are all required for a competitive approach. Product differentiation, low operating costs, customer attention, or a combination of these components can all be used to create a competitive strategy.

The steps for developing a strategy are as follows:

1) select a few significant aspects of the existing scenario;

2) examine the key strategic considerations and rate their attractiveness;

3) Create new strategies based on the identified and assessed factors.

A good strategy discovers elements of distinction or uniqueness to establish a long-term competitive advantage. It's critical to think about both internal and external elements while formulating a strategy. Personnel, economics, and technology are examples of internal factors. Economic conditions, demographics, and competitiveness are examples of external forces. Successful businesses frequently employ a plan to remain ahead of the competition and increase profits. A great strategy gives your organization a framework for making decisions, and it should be based on your consumers' needs. It engages your entire team, from leadership to sales and account management, in its creation. A strategy directs how an organization employs its resources to achieve its goals.

FORTY IS THE OLD AGE OF YOUTH;
FIFTY THE YOUTH OF OLD AGE.

Victor Hugo

Strategy development

Key questions

Current issues — Where are the ASIS organizational problems?

Target state — Where does the business want to be in the market?

Best in class — What does the business do best?

Direction — Where is the firm headed?

"TOBE" policies — What policies to define to get firm to the "TO BE" state

Success measures — How to measure strategy success?

Objectives — What are the growth and financial goal?

Leadership — Are leadership engaged with the strategy?

Customers — How to bring customers closer to the business?

Growth — How to Identify opportunities for growth & innovation?

Options — What are the strategic business opportunities?

Events — What economic & tech events that could impact the firm?

Market — What's the buying habits & behaviors of the customers?

Opportunities — How best to leverage new opportunities?

Business goals questions

Financials — To increase earnings?

Market — To increase market share?

Customers — To improve customer perception / retention?

Costs — To attain lower operational costs?

Technology — To achieve superiority using technology innovation?

Services — To lead in products & services?

Situation analysis

Internal organizational factors
- What is the organization's internal situation?
- What are business strengths and weaknesses?
- What are the capability gaps in the organization?

Technology platforms — What are the right technology platforms / development methodologies / security for business scale, speed and flexibility?

Operational processes — How to transform operational processes to keep pace with the change of customer needs and behaviors?

Marketing — What is the most effective marketing activities?

Data driven decision making
- How to improve use of data driven decision making?
- Does data support the business strategic needs?

Employee experience — How to attract and retain talent within organization?-

Workflows — How to build strategic business process workflows that are automated, intelligent and efficient?

Existing programs and projects — Are existing initiatives being reviewed for alignment with strategic objectives and if not, stopped?

Architectures — Is the business architecture aligned with the technology / security architecture?

External factors
- What are the opportunities?
- What are the threats?
- What are the success factors?

Continuous change — How to foster a culture of continuous improvement?

Competition analysis

Competition
- What are the competitors doing?
- Who uses identical technological approaches?

Competitors strategies
- What are the current strategies of competitors?
- What are the strengths and weaknesses of each competitor?

Digital competitors — Understand the best approach and activities on how to take on digital competitors.

Competitive advantage — How to create competitive advantages and deliver them in the form of technology solutions that increases efficiency and brings the customer closer to the business?

50 Emotional Intelligence

Emotional intelligence is a crucial leadership skill, and a leader must be skilled at managing their connections effectively. Being the leader of a group of people necessitates a close relationship with those individuals. EI is a long-term process that takes time to develop.

Emotional Intelligence is a difficult concept to grasp. It's all part of having the ability to make judgments that produce good results and being recognised for them. While developing emotional intelligence takes time, it is a talent that can be learned and improved through time.

Emotional intelligence teaches people how to regulate their emotions in a constructive way, how to see the difference between strategy and tactics, and how to govern themselves and their behaviours toward others.

Anyone aspiring to positions of leadership or management should work to improve their EI to build productive relationships with the people they lead, which will result in loyalty and trust. A leader who understands how to control his or her followers' emotions is more effective than one who does not. Leaders must be able to apply the EI abilities of cooperation, teamwork, and self-control effectively.

Being a successful leader entails more than just possessing the requisite skills and abilities. It necessitates that you establish a rapport with those you lead to be perceived to be able. Good leaders can successfully manage their relationships, which requires creating trust and winning respect.

Emotional Intelligence improves self-awareness to the point that you can predict your emotional reaction to situations and, if necessary, change your perspective and behaviour. Low self-awareness can lead to a slew of errors as you react without thinking, resulting in unfavourable outcomes for others around you.

TRUTH IS EVER TO BE FOUND IN
SIMPLICITY, AND NOT IN THE MULTIPLICITY
AND CONFUSION OF THINGS.

Isaac Newton

Emotional intelligence

Leader emotional intelligence

Motivation
Leaders are inspiring, not afraid of difficult stuff, focused and driven. They have focus and goals and set high standards to achieve

Self
Leaders are confident, honest, direct, consistent. They are aware of their strengths and weaknesses, and strive for continuous improvement. Making sound decisions understanding their feelings affect their judgment

Self regulation
They are clear, decisive, straight forward and intuitive. Leaders self-regulate to stay calm and manage their emotions in challenging times. Leaders who make impulsive decisions or fail to control their emotions and lash out can quickly lose the respect of their employees and stakeholders

Social skills
Good leaders are effective communicators, approachable and listen to others and understand that they need to be flexible and adaptable. Emotionally intelligent leaders who understand their employees can immediately pick up the tone of a team and can speak with honesty & sincerity to match the tone

Empathy
They have the skill show empathy when their difficult challenges and changes to face in the organisation. Leaders, with this empathy places them in their employees' shoes, thus leading to more thoughtful and deliberate decisions

Emotional intelligence is important

EI is fundamental to good leadership
A successful leader has the ability to understand those around them, as well as being aware of their own strengths and weaknesses. A leader with EI is better positioned to build meaningful relationships, both with staff & stakeholders

Makes team members feel included
Successful leaders with high EI involve make their team feel included by feeling safe, appreciated and satisfied in their work. Such leaders welcome & encourage input and feedback from staff

Understands people
Good leaders understand people; how they work, how to influence them, and how to inspire them

The benefits of emotional intelligence

Improved teamwork
A leader with EI can help their team work better together. They have good comm skills, trust and value each other's input.

Helps with change
A leader with good EI can help staff deal with change in a positive way and can inspire them to feel the same way

Handling difficult situations
A leader with EI skills, can handle conversations with upset staff or stakeholders by emotionally connecting with the other person before finding a resolution

Build trust with people
EI allows a leader to quickly build trust and rapport with their employees, by understanding their feelings & empathizing with them!

Ways to improve emotional intelligence

Take an EI test
A leader needs to take an EI test to measure their EQ (many online EQ tests)

Self observation
A leader has to be aware of their feelings. Managing emotions is easier once recognized

Question views
A leader with an high EQ see things from other people's perspectives and respect others' ideas

Take a pause
A good leader controls their emotions, maintains their composure and avoids outbursts & decides the best response to someone

An outside view
Leaders ask others for persona; feedback. If difficult accepting feedback, possible area of EI improvement

Emotional triggers
Leaders who are EI self aware, know their triggers that can initiate feelings of anger, hostility, or irritation. EI is a process that takes a long time to develop

Examples of emotional intelligence in the workplace

Bad days
Compassion & empathy is a sign of EI in practice when a leader responds positively to staff having a bad day

People in meetings
If a leader and others listen to each other respectfully in meetings, this is a good sign of Emotional Intelligence

Embracing change
How change is managed and responded to will say a lot about a leader and their relationships with employees

Flexibility
An EI leader understand the changing demands of others and is prepared to work with them on a flexible basis

Creativity
Staff are empowered & allowed the time, space, and freedom to be creative in an EI organization .

Social outside work
Employees socializing outside work and building bonds is a Sign off a emotionally intelligent workplace

51 High Performing Teams

Organizations all over the world are transforming to become teams. These groups make the most of each individual's skills and ability to continuously outperform the competition. Workgroups produce a win-win situation. High-performance work teams are built on the foundation of teamwork. Clear goals and expectations, mutual trust and respect, open communications, constructive conflict resolution, effective leadership, and team-building activities are all distinguishing features.

High-performing teams are capable of collaborating, innovating, and continuously delivering exceptional results. There is no alternative for collaboration, ingenuity, and teamwork when it comes to going above and beyond. An organisation may achieve greater heights than ever before with the right people in the appropriate roles. A high-performance team combines varied abilities and cross-functional experience to consistently create outstanding results.

A high-performance work team is an effective team. A high-performance team, on the other hand, is more than just a group of skilled and talented individuals. High performance balances individual accountability and collective achievement by driving toward a common goal with a sense of urgency. A high-performing team is well-directed and focused on adding value.

The key to effective teamwork is to take care when defining roles and responsibilities, to be open and honest with one another at all times, and to welcome constructive challenges throughout working together.

When it comes to delivering results, high-performing teams prioritise quality and creativity over efficiency, and every member embraces high-performing team principles such as collaboration, innovation, and quality, as well as a willingness to take risks to produce remarkable results.

THE FUTURE DEPENDS ON WHAT WE
DO IN THE PRESENT.

Gandhi

High performing teams

High performance team attributes

Clear goals
They have a set of clear goals aligned closely to team and organizational priorities

Roles and responsibilities
A high performance team has defined roles and responsibilities

Effective decision making
Using a mix of rational and intuitive decision making methods, depending on the task

Mutual trust
They have mutual trust and respect each other

Focus on priorities
They manage and prioritize their work and deadlines based on priorities

Participative leadership
Using a democratic leadership style that involves and engages team members

Continuous learning
A high performance team has a continuous learning mindset

Organizational goals alignment
Understand how their work aligns with organizational strategy and goals

Value diversity
A team with a diversity of experience & viewpoints, leading to better decision making

Good communications
They communicate clearly and respectfully with each other and others outside their team

Celebrate success
They celebrate success together and recognize their contributions and achievements

Positive atmosphere
An overall team culture that is transparent, positive, future-focused on success

Ways to build a high performing team

Identify shared purpose of team
A powerful way of increasing a sense of collective identity is to actively engage all members in building a shared vision

Set realistic goals
To build a high-performing team, a leader and the team members need to create feasible prioritized SMART goals

Be a good leader
A high performance team (like a racing car needs a good driver) needs a leader who has the characteristics of a good leader

Identify how to create a shared team purpose
Provide opportunities and empowerment for team members to contribute their ideas, suggestions and expertise and be valued

Employee recognition
Employees usually work harder when there work, value and contribution is visibly recognized and celebrated

Effective communications
Effective employee communications are critical to making sure everyone completes their responsibilities & collaborates together

Build team potency
Using these processes, leaders can produce a strong sense of team belief that the team can cope with challenges

Address conflicts quickly
Conflicts within high performance teams are inevitable and conflicts need to be addressed as quickly as possible.

Employee development
High performance teams require ongoing training they can develop their skills, and take on new roles within the team

The reasons teams fail

- Ineffective senior team
- A lack of a shared purpose
- A lack of taking calculated risks
- Unclear strategy
- A lack of accountability
- A lack of effective leadership
- Conflicting priorities
- Inability to deal with conflict quickly
- A lack of trust & communications
- Wrong leadership style
- Ineffective dealing with issues
- Unsure of shared team role

Leader actions for high performance

inspire
Leaders who want high-performance needs to create energy in their teams

Create stretch goals
Leaders should set stretch goals to create an internal drive in the team to make the impossible happen

Promote trust
Trust in the leader is the foundation and if not trusted they can't be inspiring to embrace goals

Communicate the vision
Leaders need to constantly communicate and keep people focused on the goals and vision

Resolve conflicts quickly
Conflicts can tear a high performance team apart if they are not resolved quickly in a mature way

52 Improve Focus & Effectiveness

Productivity isn't something that happens by chance. Many successful people have developed their method of focusing on their duties until they are completed, which has aided them in being the accomplished individuals they are today. Getting everything done that you need and want to do takes preparation and planning, as well as a steady source of desire and focus. Focus enhances communication, self-confidence, and self-esteem, as well as the ability to make sound decisions. It also improves the quality of creative work. Concentration is the ability to devote all of your attention or mind to a single task or activity at a time.

Many successful people have developed their method of focusing on their duties until they are completed, which has aided them in being the accomplished individuals they are today. Concentration is essential for improving focus and efficiency. It allows a person to develop their thoughts and adopt a unique point of view. Focus promotes inner peace and aids in the making of sound decisions and producing creative work.

The ability to focus on a specific job is crucial. People who can concentrate are better equipped to think creatively and make sound decisions, as well as try new things and gain new abilities. The capacity to concentrate is especially crucial for individuals who want to make the most of their time, whether that means being more productive at work or enjoying leisure activities more. Unfortunately, concentration is one of the most difficult abilities to perfect, and even the most accomplished individuals occasionally falter. Take control of your time and energy by learning what to prioritize and what to ignore.

IT IS SURMOUNTING DIFFICULTIES THAT
MAKES HEROES.

Louis Pasteur

Improve focus & effectiveness

Focus tips

- **Assess yourself** — Assess your mental focus now
- **No distractions** — Find place - no noise, people, F/Book
- **Prepare brain for focus** — Take a few minutes out before focus
- **Stay in the present** — Leave worries & dreams at the door
- **Take breaks** — Use Pomodoro timer for 25 min sessions & breaks
- **Mindfulness** — Start day with clearing your mind (meditation)
- **Set daily focus goals** — Break up goals into smaller tasks
- **Use Pareto 80/20 focus** — Identify 20% focus - give 80% results
- **Focus is mental exercise** — The more focus, the better you will be at focusing
- **Visualize your focus** — Before starting, visualise task
- **Physical Exercise** — It is said, exercise good for brain
- **Read paperback books** — Reading real books(not eBooks) improves focus
- **Best time for focus** — Everyone has different best times
- **Make focus a daily habit** — Focus is easier if you make it a habit
- **Reward your focus** — Reward yourself for focus sprints
- **Put had tasks first** — A good strategy, do difficult tasks first
- **Plan focus before night** — Be able to start focus immediately
- **Think big picture** — Use your big goals to drive focus
- **Positive feelings for focus** — Negative thoughts will stop your focus
- **Build distraction list** — List distractions that hinder focus
- **Tiredness** — Need to make get enough sleep
- **Stress & worries** — Stress & worries hinders good focus
- **Stop analysis paralysis** — Stop thinking about it, just do it
- **Use a journal** — Writing down helps to remove worries
- **Learn to say 'No'** — Say no to people distractions
- **Pace your focus** — Aim for consistent regular focus
- **Schedule time for focus** — Plan focus and schedule time for it
- **Each focus has a goal** — Have a goal for each focus sprint
- **Avoid procrastination** — Avoid procrastination with focus time
- **Know where to focus** — Good focus is to know where best
- **Log out of email** — For focus time, log out of internet
- **Check environment** — If too cold or hot can hinder focus
- **Doodle to improve focus** — Doodling is a good focus activity
- **No multitasking** — Focus on one thing at a time
- **Emotional stress impact** — Like normal stress, it impacts focus

Career

- **Plan career** — Plan career with priorities & goals
- **Lead a kaizen life** — Take small daily steps to improve self
- **Rise early** — Get up early & start work before everyone else
- **Take action** — Goals are dreams unless you take action
- **Keep learning** — Read every day to learn something new
- **Knowledge** — Share knowhow & experience with others
- **No limits** — Believe all is possible if you focus hard enough
- **Keep real** — Keep dreams and goals realistic
- **Time wasters** — Like negative people avoid time wasters
- **Network** — Successful people value sharing of ideas
- **Focus beyond** — To succeed, focus beyond your own role
- **Visibility** — Make sure your efforts are visible within the firm
- **Goal review** — Review your goals daily to check for progress
- **Incomes** — Aim to have more than one income source
- **Be a leader** — Leaders leverage know how of others

Self

- **Relax time** — Take some chill out time
- **Be not a victim** — Be 100% responsible and be accountable, no excuses,
- **Exercise** — Leaders make daily exercise a priority
- **Enough sleep** — Good sleep is key for good thinking
- **Self care** — Leaders have self care as a top priority for maximum performance
- **Keep balance** — Keep priorities & values in balance
- **Live in the present** — The time is now, take action now
- **Be prudent** — Wealthy people are not wasteful
- **Adapt and change** — If something does not work, change it to work
- **You have 1 mouth, 2 ears** — Nature knew the real importance of listening

53 Communication Skills

In business, communication is crucial to success. Working with your peers, subordinates, and seniors can all benefit from this basic skill. Better communication skills lead to more cohesive teams and a more enjoyable workplace. It has always been critical for our careers and relationships to be able to convey our views, opinions, and desires. It's what allows you to get along with others and accomplish amazing things together.

More than merely exchanging information is required for effective communication. It's all about deciphering the emotion and motivations underlying the data. You must be able to clearly communicate a message as well as listen in such a way that you grasp the entire meaning of what is being said and make the other person feel heard and understood. The skill of communicating ideas, facts, perspectives, and feelings from one person to another is known as communication.

Communication is the way by which businesses coordinate their activities and interact with their employees, customers, and other stakeholders

Communication aids in the accurate and rapid comprehension of information. It has always been crucial for your work and relationships to be able to explain our views, opinions, and wishes. It also helps others understand you better, which fosters interpersonal trust.

We have a greater understanding of people and situations when we communicate effectively. It assists us in overcoming differences, establishing trust and respect, and fostering the exchange of creative ideas and problem-solving opportunities. Successful communication can strengthen personal and professional relationships. They can help us understand people and circumstances that occur on a daily basis in our personal lives.

THE ART OF BEING WISE IS KNOWING
WHAT TO OVERLOOK.

William James

Communication skills

Comms are important
- **Career success** — Good comms skills is a key for a successful career
- **Leadership success** — Effective comms skills is a key skill
- **Build relationships** — Good comms fosters relations between you & your peers

Comms skills
- Confidence
- Respect
- Open mindedness
- Friendliness
- Voice tone
- Empathy
- Emotional intelligence
- Listening
- Asking questions
- Clarity

Listening skills
- **Appreciative listening** — Listen to someone speaking because you enjoy it like it
- **Emphatic listening** — Listening empathically shows mutual concern to identify with speaker's situation
- **Comprehensive listening** — Listening to a lecture you want to comprehend what is being said
- **Critical listening** — Listening closely to understand the results & possible impacts
  - Face speaker & keep eye contact
  - Don't interrupt
  - Keep an open mind
  - Pay attention to non-verbal clues
  - Be attentive but relaxed
  - Don't impose your solutions
  - Listen and try to picture what the person is saying
  - Wait for speaker to pause before asking questions
  - Give speaker regular feedback
  - Try to feel what speaker is saying

Email etiquette
- **A specific subject** — Title your email so recipient immediately knows topic
- **Start with a greeting** — Personalise by including the recipient's name
- **Choose your words carefully** — Choose your words carefully in your emails very careful. Don't write anything to taken the wrong way or can hurt you in future
- **Check spelling** — This is a basic no-brainer for quality
- **No emoticons** — Keep them for friends
- **Make it personable** — Start message off on a positive note
- **Leave off or handle attachments** — Leave them off or paste in email
- **End with a closing** — End email with a good closing
- **Keep business emails professional** — Keep emails professional in style, & take care using grammar points
- **End email with a call to action** — End your email with a call to action. Set expectation of what response & when
- **Be clear about purpose of email** — Be clear about purpose email, & ask specific questions to be answered
- **Don't ramble** — Focus getting the basic points across that person needs to know

Effective meetings
- **An agenda** — Have an agenda with clear aims
- **Time limit** — Set an end time & stick to it
- **Relevant attendees** — Invite only relevant people to the meeting
- **Meeting facilitator** — Have a facilitator & someone to record decisions & actions
- **Go meeting lean** — Go lean to reduce wasteful meetings
- **Accountability** — Create action items with accountability

Presenting ideas
- **Your boss** — How does your boss like data presented?
- **Past examples** — Bosses don't like risks, support idea with past examples
- **Make you idea engaging** — Aim to leave a lasting impression by using a story or example that makes idea memorable
- **Research idea** — Back up idea with quantifiable metrics
- **Highlight benefits** — Show the what, the why and benefits of idea
- **Present costs** — Present costs for idea in a visual way & business impact

Difficult situations
- **Establish the facts** — Facts as opposed to opinion
- **Ask questions** — When issue arise? Impact?
- **Gather data** — Gather staff data
- **Actively lesson** — Pay attention to what is said
- **Remain professional** — Remain professional
- **Win-win** — Aim for win-win

Performance reviews
- **Reviews** — Make time for reviews
- **Active listener** — Be an active listener
- **Choose words carefully** — Avoid confrontational words
- **Get prepared for review** — Prepare notes and agenda
- **Align on expectations** — Align on expectations for staff
- **Focus on the future** — Focus on future not the past
- **Ask the right questions** — Ask the right questions
- **End with agreed next steps** — End the review - next steps
- **Schedule follow-up** — Schedule follow-up meeting

54 Mentoring Skills

Having a mentor can be one of the most life-changing experiences. Mentorship is a highly enjoyable and productive experience that helps both parties reach their professional objectives more quickly. Mentorship is a semi-structured guidance system in which one person contributes their knowledge, abilities, and experience to help others advance in their careers. A mentor is a tutor, coach, or co-worker who has experience in one or more of your areas of interest and can help you figure out how to get there. These mentors are experts in their fields and have worked with career development before, so they can create a learning environment that is suited to your personal needs. They may assist you in overcoming roadblocks on your way to professional achievement and navigating you to the next level of your career.

A mentor is usually a seasoned professional in the same area who acts as a role model and advisor. Mentoring helps people build new responsibilities, networks, and relationships, which helps them advance in their careers. It aids in the identification of strengths and weaknesses as well as the development of a more diverse skill set. The sharing of knowledge, experience, and expertise is what mentoring is all about. A mentor or mentee is someone who learns from someone more experienced or competent, usually in an organised relationship with structured feedback. Professional skills, personal growth, and general life counsel are examples of content that vary based on the scenario and context of the interaction. Mentor will help you with promoting your items, positioning yourself for promotion, delivering a better presentation, managing your budget properly, and much more.

WHEN YOU ARISE IN THE MORNING, THINK
OF WHAT A PRECIOUS PRIVILEGE IT IS TO
BE ALIVE - TO BREATHE, TO THINK, TO
ENJOY, TO LOVE.

Marcus Aurelius

Mentoring skills

Mentoring purpose
- **Mentoring is giving more than advice** — Or passing on what your experience was in a particular area. It's about motivating the other person to identify their own issues & aims
- **Not counselling or therapy** — It is not counselling or therapy, though a mentor can help the mentee access help
- **Short term or long term** — Mentoring can be a short-term arrangement or it can last years
- **Knowhow** — Share firm knowhow

Mentoring is important
- **Share new skills** — Impart new skills
- **Professional growth** — Support professional growth
- **Staff loyalty** — Boost staff loyalty
- **Future leaders** — Develop new leaders
- **Onboarding** — An onboarding tool

Mentoring approaches
- **Traditional one to one mentoring** — Mentee-mentor partners participate in a relationship with structure and timeframe of their own making
- **Distance mentoring** — Mentoring in which the two parties are in different locations called "virtual" mentoring
- **Group mentoring** — A mentor is matched with group of mentees and directs progress & activities

Mentoring techniques
- **Accompanying** — Making a commitment which involves taking part in the learning process side-by-side with the learner
- **Catalysing** — When change reaches a critical level of pressure, learning can escalate. The mentor chooses to plunge learner right into change
- **Showing** — This is making something understandable to demonstrate a skill. You show what you are talking about, you show by your own behaviour
- **Sowing** — Mentors are often confronted with the difficulty of preparing the learner before they are ready to change. Sowing is used when what you say may not be understood at first pass
- **Harvesting** — Here the mentor focuses on "picking the ripe fruit": it is usually used to create awareness of what was learned & to draw conclusions.

Different types of mentors
- **Professional mentor** — They know the new practices that helps a person's role
- **Multiple mentors** — Multiple mentors will widen a persons knowledge
- **Industry mentor** — A mentor will give insight on the industry
- **Organizational mentor** — They know the politics, values, strategies & products
- **Work process mentor** — Explains the 'ins and outs' of day to day tasks
- **Technology mentor** — Advise on systems and on new technologies

Mentoring program
- **Career development program** — A career development mentoring program for employees helps junior employees to learn the skills and behaviours from senior staff
- **High potential mentoring program** — A mentoring program for high-potential employees from leaders helps to develop top performing employees & increase retention
- **Diversity mentoring program** — Mentors from underrepresented groups can help staff from underrepresented groups have confidence to take new roles

Qualities of a good mentor
- **Share knowledge** — Share skills, know how & expertise
- **Positive role model** — Acts as a positive role model
- **Shows enthusiasm** — Shows enthusiasm for the role of mentoring
- **Value ongoing learning** — Values continuous learning and ongoing growth in the field
- **Provides feedback** — Gives constructive feedback
- **Values others** — Values the opinions of others
- **Motivates others** — By setting a good example as a role model
- **Takes interest in relationship** — Takes a personal interest in the mentoring relationship
- **Meets professional goals** — Use mentoring to meet ongoing personal and professional goals
- **Respected by colleagues** — Mentees want to follow someone respected

Mentoring tips
- **Needs assessment** — Ask mentee about their priorities
- **Set expectations** — Set expectations & ground rules
- **Listen, then ask, then advise** — Don't drone on about your own brilliance, listen to the mentee
- **Check your biases & impulses** — Don't let stereotypes distort your impressions of a mentee
- **Create schedule** — Create a contact schedule
- **Set goals mutually** — Ask mentee manager what goals?
- **Be accountable** — Be accountable to each other
- **Open doors** — Use connections to open doors for mentee
- **Let mentees make own decisions** — Let them make their own decisions
- **Be realistic** — Have an honest discussion of what you can do for a mentee

55 Essential Soft Skills

According to research, your capacity to keep a happy mood and complete tasks is closely related to your business success. Interpersonal skills enable professionals to effectively communicate with a wide range of people at work, including clients or customers, supervisors or managers, team members, and others. These abilities include paying attention to nonverbal communication features and are considered the cornerstone for successful relationships.

Essential soft skills are a set of best practices for improving your work performance. Successful people have self-control and interpersonal skills that are essential for staying on track and interacting well with others. These basic behavioural abilities on relationships with team members, staying on schedule, managing stress, and persisting through adversities are what employers are looking for in new workers.

There are a variety of interpersonal, self-regulatory, and task-related abilities that are linked to good workplace performance. Through successful interactions, stress control, and consistent effort, these behavioural skills help professionals succeed.

Behavioural talents are divided into three categories.

1. Interpersonal behaviour skills, which include knowing how one's behaviours affect workplace relationships and how to project a pleasant attitude.

2. Self-Regulatory Behaviours Skills are designed to help people cope with stressful situations and difficult jobs by shifting their perceptions and viewpoints.

3. Task-Related Information Individuals learn how to operate effectively as members of a team, find techniques for managing clients and customers, and approach work with a sense of professional accountability through the development of behavioural skills.

A leader can use self-assessments to figure out which important abilities in different areas of business comms they need to work on.

OUT OF YOUR VULNERABILITIES WILL
COME YOUR STRENGTH.

Sigmund Freud

Essential soft skills

Soft skills improvement

- **Do a self assessment** — Perform a self assessment of soft skills to identify improvement areas and validate with feedback
- **A learning mindset** — Focus on improving soft skills with courses in comms, public speaking & presentations
- **Find a coach or mentor** — Identify a coach or mentor who can give advice and provide feedback on an individual's soft skills
- **Expand your mindset** — There are many videos and articles online about soft skills such as Comms and presentation skills
- **Look for opportunities** — The best way to improve presentation and public speaking skills is to practice as much as possible doing it

Creativity

- **Creative time** — To develop creative skill, time has set aside for them
- **Use mind maps** — Mind maps connect ideas and enable to look for answers
- **Walk or exercise** — Walking and exercise are great simulants for creative thoughts
- **Inspiration from others** — To find new ideas, look how other industries do things
- **Collaborate with others** — Brainstorming s is still one of the best creative way to use
- **Become an expert** — One of the best ways to become creative is to become an expert
- **Do what you love** — Love and creativity are joined at the hips, do something you love
- **Use connections** — A good creative technique is to look for connections between topics
- **In the right mood** — Many people listen to music or eat different foods for creativity
- **Use Bono six thinking hats** — Look on Google on how use De Bono Six Hats Thinking for innovative ideas

Persuasion

- **Be confident** — It is important to be and project confidence in your appeal
- **Use your strengths** — Leverage your personal strengths to maximise your persuasive skills
- **Know your audience** — A key success factor for persuading an audience is knowing their needs
- **Common ground** — Establish common ground with an audience, a good persuasion start
- **Tell a story** — A traditional way to persuade others is to share a story as part of an appeal
- **Prepared for pushback** — Good persuaders are prepared for pushback as part of persuasive plan
- **Adapt to audience** — Good persuaders can adapt to the different people personalities
- **Use logical arguments** — Use logical arguments to persuade people to support an appeal
- **Talk benefits** — Highlight benefits in your appeal / presentation to the audience
- **Leverage your track record** — People are persuaded more by people who done something before successfully

Collaboration

- **Good communications** — Good comms is a key success factor to foster collaboration with a team
- **Build trust** — Effective collaboration is build on a foundation of trust & reliability
- **Accommodate others** — For good collaboration, a team needs to able to accommodate others ideas
- **Expect conflict** — Creative teams often use conflict to reach consensus n new ideas
- **Embrace change** — An ability to embrace change can be a key factor for successful collaboration
- **Share knowledge** — Sharing knowledge & experience are great ways to foster collaboration
- **Be a team player** — Collaboration works, when every one is a team player (joint goals)
- **Have credibility** — The ability to be credible & believable is a key skill for team collaboration
- **Become a winning team** — A win team has the right players, the right attitude, & the right leader
- **Establish the right balance** — Aim for right balance between chaos and analysis paralysis & make joint decisions

Adaptability

- **Be willing to learn** — Become a continual learner for new ideas and ways of doing things
- **Be resilient** — Adaptability is closely linked to resilience and perseverance.
- **Be spontaneous** — Avoid over analysis of new ideas, embrace new opportunity to change
- **A 'can-do' person** — Leaders like to have positive "can-do" peoples in their teams
- **Refuse to be a victim** — Adopt a survival problem solving attitude to any crisis that happens in your life

Emotional intelligence

- **Self awareness** — You know how your emotions & actions can affect the people around you
- **Self regulation** — Self regulating people rarely verbally attack others, make rushed or emotional decisions
- **Motivation** — Self-motivated people work consistently toward goals, and high standards for the quality of their work
- **Empathy** — Emphatic people have the ability to put themselves in someone else's situation & listen to feedback
- **Social skills** — People with social skills are good communicators who can gain support for ideas and also handle conflict situations

Essential soft skills

Comms
- **Know you audience:** Not one size fits all in comms (people)
- **Adapt for delivery:** Adapt different learning styles
- **Clear goals:** Comms goals & follow-up is clear
- **Keep it simple:** Avoid jargon, kiss
- **Be detail aware:** Base detail & amount on context
- **Follow-up comms:** Follow up understanding: up & any questions
- **Keep comms two-way:** Comms is a 2 way process -1 mouth, 2 ears

Listening
- **Build trust & rapport:** Show interest and ask on how to help audience
- **Demonstrate empathy:** Align with their thoughts and feelings on the subject
- **Paraphrase:** Repeat what is stated in your own words to clarify understanding
- **Affirmations:** Review what's said & actions agreed
- **Ask questions:** Ask open ended and specific questions

Conflict resolution
- **Clarification:** What is the issue about between both sides?
- **Desired outcome:** What is the desired outcome of the conflict?
- **Identify ways forward:** Discuss ways to meet the desired outcome
- **Determine barriers:** Both sides agree on issue & what actions to do
- **Agree best way:** Agree way for conflict resolution for both sides
- **Solution:** Acknowledge agreed solution and roles

Negotiation
- **Preparation:** Consider approach collect data to plan an agreement
- **Agree logistics:** The place, time, rules & process for negotiation
- **Clarification & justification:** Each party clarifies and justifies demand, issues
- **Problem solving:** Discuss resolution with concessions both sides
- **Closure:** Ends with agreement for execution / monitor

Problem solving
- **Identify problem:** Clarify problem from different views
- **Understand stakeholders:** Ensure all stakeholders are included
- **List options:** Identify and list solution options
- **Evaluate options:** Look at pros and cons for option
- **Select option:** Select best solution options
- **Document solution:** The golden rule of putting it all in writing is a good one
- **Agree follow-up:** Evaluate & agree fallback option

Analytical thinking
- **Creativity:** Think outside of the box for ideas
- **Critical thinking:** Evaluate data & decide on results
- **Data analysis:** Examine data & identify trends
- **Research:** Collect data & research a topic
- **Solution development:** Develop solution based on research
- **Testing solution:** Test solution and ideas based on research and findings
- **Post analysis:** Review lessons learned

Facilitation
- 1. Plan the workshop logistics
- 2: Introductions, agenda, goals
- 3. Identify the problem to solve
- 4. Find issues & tasks
- 5 Use sticky notes for inputs
- 6. Prioritise important topics
- 7. Highlight top priorities
- 8. Discuss needs for top priorities
- 9. Decide roles & dates
- 10. Agree on next steps

Presentation
- **Analyse audience:** Audience's interests, values
- **Select topic:** Topic based on research
- **Define objectives:** Define presentation goals
- **Prepare content:** Include data, facts, quotes
- **Presentation open and close:** Create impactful open /close
- **Deliver successful presentation:** Tell them what you are going tell them, tell them & tell them what you told them
- **Practice delivery:** Present for feedback & inputs

Questioning
- Tell me about your pain points and challenges?
- What is the primary thing to change?
- What things not to change?
- If this happens, what benefits?
- If this doesn't happen, the impact?

Decision making
- **The purpose of decision:** What is the issue to solve?
- **Gather information:** Gather data to understand what needs to be done
- **Consider the impacts:** Determine the impacts to all of the stakeholders
- **Make the decision:** After this process & the impacts, make decision
- Once decision is made, monitor impacts

56 Successful Presentations

Whether you're doing an online or in-person presentation, comprehensive preparation is the most crucial aspect of delivering a great presentation. Before you give your presentation, identify your goal, prepare how you'll get there, rehearse and practise, and then deliver it with confidence. A good presentation is never given by itself. The actual topic and content of your presentation should be carefully considered. Presentations that are clear, exact, and honed are effective. You can never over-prepare for a presentation, however. Preparing for a presentation is an important element of the preparation process since it allows you to manage your anxiety and give an effective and efficient performance. Depending on the audience, the delivery method may need to change. As a result, when deciding on the material and delivery style to use, it's critical to think about your audience and their background.

Keep your schedule reasonable and include additional time in case things don't go as planned. Allow plenty of opportunities for you to practise your speaking. Deliver your presentation the night before so you may re-evaluate and make any final revisions. Otherwise, you will lose credibility if your equipment is not in good working order: technical glitches are sometimes enough to turn off an audience!

An excellent speech is similar to a well-written narrative essay. In both circumstances, you'll need a clear structure and a well-thought-out strategy for developing your argument and demonstrating the legitimacy of your point of view through evidence and appropriate examples. Furthermore, keep in mind that a good storey is made up of more than just facts, statistics, and words; it also includes things like persuasive methods and great persuasive speech.

EXPERIENCE WITHOUT THEORY IS BLIND,
BUT THEORY WITHOUT EXPERIENCE IS
MERE INTELLECTUAL PLAY.

Immanuel Kant

Successful presentations

Personal qualities

Confidence
Your confidence will help you to present to an audience. People want you to succeed & they want you to make them at ease

Use your voice effectively
By using your voice effectively & varying the speed & pitch all helps to make your voice interesting to hold attention

Naturalness
Presentations should be professional but allow yourself to be natural when presenting for a much more engaging talk

Breathe, relax and enjoy
Aim to relax yourself, you will present better. If you can start to enjoy yourself & the audience will respond to that & engage better

Passion
When you can speak passionately about a subject, it will help to hold the attention of the audience & hopefully ignite their own passion

Use the right body language to get your message across
It has been estimated that more than three quarters of communication is non-verbal. Your body language is crucial to getting your message across. Body language to avoid includes crossed arms, hands held behind your back or in your pockets, and pacing the stage

Knowledge
An audience can always tell the difference between someone who really knows their subject & those who are just regurgitating facts

Presentation qualities

Organization
To avoid confusion in the message your key points need to connect and lead from one into the other

Emotional impact
Good presentations are memorable with graphics, images, and facts in such a way that they're easy to remember

Build rapport with audience
If you smile & make eye contact, you will build rapport, which helps the audience to connect with you & helps nervousness

Focus on audience needs
During presentation preparation, always consider what the audience needs and wants to know, not what you can tell them

Good presentations are stories
Great presentations are stories. Great presentations take the audience through an emotional to decide right here, right now

Time sensitive
Keep a presentation to a reasonable length is important as your audience isn't going to listen forever, so make it as concise as possible

Motivating
Good presentations are motivating. They bring the audience members to the point where they can make a final decision on what is said

Have a strong start
The beginning of your presentation is crucial. So don't waste that on explaining who you are. Start by entertaining them to engage them

Keep it simple
A successful presentation is one where a clear, concise message that can easily be interpreted message is well delivered

Honest data in a honest way
Good presentations contain valid information. Each piece of data is thoroughly fact-checked, accurate, and never misleading

Use 10-20-30 rule
Presentation contain no more than 10 slides, to last no more than 20 minutes; and use a font size of no less than 30 point

A slideshow for you
A good rule is that a good set of slides should be no use without the presenter, and they should definitely contain less, not more

Preparation qualities

Prepare thoroughly
Good preparation will improve your confidence

Identify the key messages
When planning, ask the question "What is the key message (or three key points) for the audience to take away?"

Cut out waste to core messages
And if you are planning to say something that doesn't contribute to the core message(s), **don't say it, cut it out.** Take a Lean Principle approach to presentations, remove any non value messages i.e.. waste

Learn from others
A good practice is to learn from others. Watch TED talks on YouTube to get tips from their presentation content, skills and delivery

Start with a good story
It is a good idea to start your presentation with a story and if you need your presentation to act like a story. People respond to stories

Practice, practice, practice
Practice your presentation multiple times with a colleague as it's essential if you want to deliver a rousing presentation

Practice your passion
An enthusiastic and passionate presentation is a key to a successful one so practice being enthusiastic and energetic too

On-day preparation

Arrive early
Allow plenty of time to settle in before presentation. Extra time will allow you to adapt

Adjust to your surroundings
Practice with the microphone & make sure you know the seating & be aware of any distractions

Meet and greet your audience
Chat with people before presentation as this makes you seem more likeable. Ask questions & note their responses

Use positive visualization
Use positive visualization to see a positive outcome to the presentation

Successful online presentations

For a successful online presentation you will need an effective, efficient process and get it right the first time

Environment

Consider your environment
For an online presentation, consider your environment. Spotty Wi-Fi with an unprofessional unclean background & a poorly-lit face can kill your presentation

Quiet space
Ensure you are in a quiet space with no distractions or people moving around

Multiple screens
Consider use of multiple large screens to see all the participants

Use the right tools
Make sure to select the right tools for your online presentation

Production

Audio
Place the mic approximately 6 to 8 inches from your mouth

Video
Make sure you are in middle of the screen

Camera
Set your camera to auto-focus . Check the upper part of body & head framed

Lighting
Make sure that your lighting is adequate; face your lighting

Keep video engaging
Keep video engaging by inserting multimedia when appropriate

Preparation

Plan structure
Structure is key for online sessions & don't allow for much flexibility

Rehearse
Rehearse presentation with others' fine-tune timing, pacing & transition

Test the software
Test the software so things will work when you're ready to go live

Presenter photos
Include presenter photos to give audience an idea of who you are

Plan for interactivity
Plan for interaction with Surveys, Whiteboarding, Questions, Quizzes

Chunk content
Break presentation into 5 mins chunks broken up polls, questions and quizzes

Make it entertaining
Having lots of factual information doesn't mean it has to be dry & dull.

Keep content simple
The content must be clear & explicit (visual & design versus words)

Supporting slides
Create slides to support presentation not mimic it completely

Plan for assistance
Plan to have someone available to deal with technical issues & chats

Presenter

Use your voice
Voice inflection is the way to gesture online

Avoid use of pauses
Avoid excessive use of verbal pauses

Look directly into camera
Look into camera & speak to audience

Accessible notes
Have your notes accessible to hand

Wardrobe on video
Wardrobe best colours for video: blue, green, purple

Online tools

Kaltura: Kaltura's integration with Canvas allows to share video, audio, & images

Genially: Genial.ly enables the creation of interactive image, and presentations

Poll everywhere: This can be used to ask audience for feedback & can help gauge audience's understanding

Engagement

Engage the audience
For online presentations, you have to engage your audience so avoid droning on

Start on time with a welcome exercise
Start on time! Include a welcome exercise to establish rapport with audience

Tell a story, ask a question, do a straw poll
Break up your presentation to regularly to tell a quick story, ask a question, take a straw poll, tell a joke!

Presentation

Set expectations
Tell audience to participate & how to ask questions and when

One idea per slide
No more than 3-4 bullets if possible

One minute per slide
Use more slides, with less content per slide

Use a handouts
Use handouts if there is a lot of text to disseminate

Allow others to speak
A variety of voices is good for interest & engagement

Transitions are critical
You must connect what you just said to what is coming next

Imagine your audience
A tip is to place pictures of audience members behind your camera

Encourage audience to access webinar in advance
So any tech issues can be dealt in advance & familiarise them with the technology used

Avoid quickness
Avoid quickly moving cursors, polls, windows

Plan for interactivity
Plan interactivity every 3 to 5 minutes & ensure it's on topic. Have someone help you follow the chats

Incorporate chat inputs into presentation
Incorporate contributed material from the chat into presentation

57 Stakeholder Management

Stakeholder management identifies the people who are most interested in or affected by the actions of a program. These persons must be aware of the program's current status, as well as its future goals and objectives, significant operational changes, shortcomings, strengths, and achievements. To do this, continual communication with all stakeholders is required, with a focus on their comprehension of the mission's impact.

Stakeholder participation is an essential component of successful program management. Stakeholder behaviour can be influenced by a variety of actions and tactics that make up stakeholder management.

Anyone who has a vested interest in or is influenced by the success of your program is referred to as a stakeholder. It might be anyone, from a major donor to end-users of whatever you're making, and anything in between.

Some people will be affected by the work in every program. These people are known as stakeholders, and there are more of them than you may think: program personnel, employees, program participants, and sponsors, to name a few.

One of the most important things a program manager / leader does is identify, communicate with, and manage the communities that a program impacts stakeholders. Stakeholders include anyone who participates in or is interested in the outcome of your program.

A program plan outlines your program's assumptions and limits, as well as the steps you'll take to achieve your goals. The program plan describes the roles, duties, relationships, and contributions of those individuals and organizations who will be affected by, contribute to or are accountable for accomplishing the specified results.

A DISCIPLINED MIND BRINGS HAPPINESS.

Gautama Buddha

Stakeholder management

Stakeholder management

Stakeholder management — The identification of stakeholders, analysis of their expectations & influences

Stakeholder management comms plan purpose — An outline of who to communicate with, how to do It & how often

Potential stakeholders — The program team, program sponsors, executives, IT, business units and suppliers

Managing expectations & requirements — The managing of the expectations and the needs of these stakeholders

Stakeholder analysis & identification — It involves identifying & analysing stakeholders & planning to communicate & engaging them

Deliver measurable results — Effective comms will help you to deliver measurable results to organization

Stakeholder management benefits

Understanding of goal — Stakeholders must understand what you are trying to achieve with program Goals

Operational effectiveness — A stakeholder communications plan can support or improve your operational effectiveness

Influencing source of power — Your comms plan must focus on the stakeholders who have the greatest influence on your success

Best practices

Know your audience — A stakeholder refers to all resources who have an interest in a project

Stakeholder management means communications — Delivering and sharing the right messages to stakeholders is essential

Take a proactive approach — Take a proactive collaborative approach to stakeholders' comms

Find the right platform — Find the PM tool for stakeholder comms, quick access & decision making

Stakeholder identification

Who will be impacted? — Who will be affected by your program?

Who has an interest? — Who has interest in the project?

Who has project influence? — Who has influence over your project?

Project to fail? — Who wants your project to fail?

Project to succeed? — Who wants your project to be successful

Stakeholder analysis

Evaluate stakeholders for power & interest — Evaluate the stakeholders in terms of their power and interest they have over the project. and the decide which stakeholders to spend most effort on

High power / high interest (fully engage) — The stakeholders you place in this are are the key players & to spend the most effort with these people

Low power / high interest (keep informed) — Provide information on the project to these people and ensure that they don't have any issues

Power interest grid — Categorise stakeholders according to power and Interest. What is the amount of power that each stakeholder has on the success of the project? Used to develop a comms plan

High power / low interest (keep satisfied) — Make enough effort to keep these stakeholders satisfied. But refrain from going overboard with your communication efforts lest you make them bored.

Low power / low interest (minimum effort) — Monitor these stakeholders and their interest in the project and provide them with adequate information without overloading them with unnecessary communications

Stakeholder planning

Create stakeholder profiles — Create a one profile for each stakeholder category should list their needs, interests, goals, role etc.

Take action to address issues — Take necessary actions to address issues or you may lose their continuous support

Key messages to communicate — The key messages to comm & engagement approach

Best comms approach — Choose most appropriate approach to stakeholders to communicate

The communication channels to use — The comms channels (e.g.: emails, newsletters, video calls etc.) and the frequency of engagement

Communication plan process

Monitor for issues — Constantly monitor them if they may have issues

Use emails/ newsletters — For minimum effort stakeholders (low power / low interest)

Monitor effectiveness — Monitor and measure effectiveness of stakeholder engagement

LIFE ISN'T ABOUT FINDING
YOURSELF.

George Bernard Shaw

Acknowledgements

One Page Concept and Contents: Ken Martin

Source of Royalty Free Quotes (pre-1923): The GoldenQuotes.Net

3 Magic Publications

Birmingham.

United Kingdom

3 Magic Publications

After an extensive successful career working for some of the best organisations in the world in various countries, I was disheartened to see how many times programs and projects failed from not paying heed to lessons learned and best practices. Even today, how many current programs are being executed without proper assessment, planning or organisational change management, And then organisations are surprised why so many of the programs and projects fail to deliver any business benefits.

I decided to author and to create several Best Practice Books based on my **One Page Magic**™ format on topics such as PMO, Project Management & Business Transformation for leaders to learn from other's experience for project success. When opportunities arise, I collaborate with others to capture their knowledge, experience and best practices to produce additional best practices books.

Other Publications on Amazon

OPM best practices handbooks
- PMO handbook
- Transformation handbook
- Transformational leadership handbook
- CIO handbook
- CTO handbook

One page magic series
- PMO magic
- Transformation magic
- PM magic
- Opex magic
- Leader magic
- Agile magic
- Career magic

The OPM demystified series
- PMO demystified
- PM demystified

The OPM 8-minute series
- CIO/ CTO guide
- DT/ CX guide
- Agile guide
- PMO setup guide
- Live your future guide
- Career guide
- Program planning guide
- Operational excellence guide
- Leadership guide
- Fintech guide
- Disruptive tech guide
- Transformation PMO guide
- PMO governance guide

The magic megabook series
- The transformation magic megabook
- The PMO magic megabook

Printed in Great Britain
by Amazon

23433418R00117